Vocabulary Power Plus for the New SAT:

Vocabulary, Reading, and Writing Exercises for High Scores

Book Two

By Daniel A. Reed

Edited by Paul Moliken

ISBN 978-1-58049-254-6

Revised March, 2012

P.O. Box 658 · Clayton, DE 19938
(800) 932-4593 · www.prestwickhouse.com

Table of Contents

INTRODUCTION

Vocabulary Power Plus for the New SAT combines classroom-tested vocabulary drills with reading and writing exercises designed to prepare students for the revised Scholastic Assessment Test; however, *Vocabulary Power Plus for the New SAT* is a resource for all students—not just those who are college bound or preparing for the SAT I. This series is intended to increase vocabulary, improve grammar, enhance writing, and boost critical reading skills for students at all levels of learning.

Critical Reading exercises include lengthy passages and detailed questions. We use SAT-style grammar and writing exercises and have placed the vocabulary words in a non-alphabetical sequence.

To reflect the changes to the Writing and Critical Reading portions of the SAT I, Prestwick House includes inferential exercises instead of the analogical reasoning sections. Coupled with words-in-context activities, inferences cultivate comprehensive word discernment by prompting students to create contexts for words instead of simply memorizing definitions.

The writing exercises in *Vocabulary Power Plus for the New SAT* are process-oriented, but they bring students a step closer to SAT success by exposing them to rubrics that simulate those of the SAT essay-writing component. This exposure to an objective scoring process helps students to develop a concrete understanding of writing fundamentals.

We hope that you find the *Vocabulary Power Plus for the New SAT* series to be an effective tool for teaching new words and an exceptional tool for preparing for the new SAT.

Strategies for Completing Activities

Roots, Prefixes, and Suffixes

A knowledge of roots, prefixes, and suffixes can give readers the ability to view unfamiliar words as puzzles that require only a few simple steps to solve. For the person interested in the history of words, this knowledge provides the ability to track word origin and evolution. For those who seek to improve vocabulary, this knowledge creates a sure and lifelong method; however, there are two points to remember:

1. Some words have evolved through usage, so present definitions might differ from what you infer through an examination of the roots and prefixes. The word *abstruse*, for example, contains the prefix *ab* (away) and the root *trudere* (to thrust), and literally means *to thrust away*. Today, *abstruse* is used to describe something that is hard to understand.

2. Certain roots do not apply to all words that use the same form. If you know that the root *vin* means "to conquer," then you would be correct in concluding that the word *invincible* means "incapable of being conquered"; however, if you tried to apply the same root meaning to *vindicate* or *vindictive*, you would be incorrect. When analyzing unfamiliar words, check for other possible roots if your inferred meaning does not fit the context.

Despite these considerations, a knowledge of roots and prefixes is one of the best ways to build a powerful vocabulary.

Critical Reading

Reading questions generally fall into several categories.

1. *Identifying the main idea or the author's purpose.* Generally, the question will ask, "What is this selection about?"

In some passages, the author's purpose will be easy to identify because the one or two ideas leap from the text; however, other passages might not be so easily analyzed, especially if they include convoluted sentences. Inverted sentences (subject at the end of the sentence) and elliptical sentences (words missing) will also increase the difficulty of the passages, but all of these obstacles can be overcome if readers take one sentence at a time and recast it in their own words. Consider the following sentence:

> These writers either jot down their thoughts bit by bit, in short, ambiguous, and paradoxical sentences, which apparently mean much more than they say—of this kind of writing Schelling's treatises on natural philosophy are a splendid instance; or else they hold forth with a deluge of words and the most intolerable diffusiveness, as though no end of fuss were necessary to make the reader understand the deep meaning of their sentences, whereas it is some quite simple if not actually trivial idea, examples of which may be found in plenty in the popular works of Fichte, and the philosophical manuals of a hundred other miserable dunces.

If we edit out some of the words, the main point of this sentence is obvious.

> These writers either jot down their thoughts bit by bit, in short,
> sentences, which apparently mean
> much more than they say
> or
> they hold a deluge of words
> as though necessary to make the
> reader understand the deep meaning of their sentences

Some sentences need only a few deletions for clarification, but others require major recasting and additions; they must be read carefully and put into the reader's own words.

> Some in their discourse desire rather commendation of wit, in being able to hold all arguments, than of judgment, in discerning what is true; as if it were a praise to know what might be said, and not what should be thought.

After studying it, a reader might recast the sentence as follows:

> In conversation, some people desire praise for their abilities to maintain the conversation rather than their abilities to identify what is true or false, as though it were better to sound good than to know what is truth or fiction.

2. Identifying the stated or implied meaning. *What is the author stating or suggesting?*

The literal meaning of a text does not always correspond with the intended meaning. To understand a passage fully, readers must determine which meaning—if there is more than one—is the intended meaning of the passage.

Consider the following sentence:

> If his notice was sought, an expression of courtesy and interest gleamed out upon his features; proving that there was light within him and that it was only the outward medium of the intellectual lamp that obstructed the rays in their passage.

Interpreted literally, this Nathaniel Hawthorne metaphor suggests that a light-generating lamp exists inside of the human body. Since this is impossible, the reader must look to the metaphoric meaning of the passage to properly understand it. In the metaphor, Hawthorne refers to the human mind—consciousness—as a lamp that emits light, and other people cannot always see the lamp because the outside "medium"—the human body—sometimes blocks it.

3. Identifying the tone or mood of the selection. *What feeling does the text evoke?*

To answer these types of questions, readers must look closely at individual words and their connotations; for example, the words *stubborn* and *firm* have almost the same definition, but a writer who describes a character as *stubborn* rather than *firm* is probably suggesting something negative about the character.

Writing

The new SAT allocates only twenty-five minutes to the composition of a well-organized, fully developed essay. Writing a satisfactory essay in this limited time requires the ability to quickly determine a thesis, organize ideas, and produce adequate examples to support the ideas.

An essay written in twenty minutes might not represent the best process writing—an SAT essay might lack the perfection and depth that weeks of proofreading and editing give to research papers. Process is undoubtedly important, but students must consider the time constraints of the SAT. Completion of the essay is just as important as organization, development, and language use.

The thesis, the organization of ideas, and the support make the framework of a good essay. Before the actual writing begins, writers must create a mental outline by establishing a thesis, or main idea, and one or more specific supporting ideas (the number of ideas will depend on the length and content of the essay). Supporting ideas should not be overcomplicated; they are simply ideas that justify or explain the thesis. The writer must introduce and explain each supporting idea, and the resultant supporting paragraph should answer the *why?* or *who cares?* questions that the thesis may evoke.

Once the thesis and supporting ideas are identified, writers must determine the order in which the ideas will appear in the essay. A good introduction usually explains the thesis and briefly introduces the supporting ideas. Explanation of the supporting ideas should follow, with each idea in its own paragraph. The final paragraph, the conclusion, usually restates the thesis or summarizes the main ideas of the essay.

Adhering to the mental outline when the writing begins will help the writer organize and develop the essay. Using the Organization and Development scoring guides to evaluate practice essays will help to reinforce the process skills. The Word Choice and Sentence Formation scoring guides will help to strengthen language skills—the vital counterpart to essay organization and development.

Pronunciation Guide

a — tr**a**ck
ā — m**a**te
ä — f**a**ther
â — c**a**re
e — p**e**t
ē — b**e**
i — b**i**t
ī — b**i**te
o — j**o**b
ō — wr**o**te
ô — p**o**rt, h**o**rse, f**ough**t
ōō — pr**oo**f
ŏŏ — b**oo**k
u — p**u**n
ū — **you**
û — p**u**rr
ə — **a**bout, syst**e**m, s**u**pper, circ**u**s
îr — st**eer**
ë — Fr. c**oeu**r
oi — t**oy**

Word List

Lesson 1
abet
coerce
divulge
dogmatic
extraneous
gregarious
insipid
jaundiced
meticulous
temerity

Lesson 2
anathema
banter
castigate
docile
emaciated
gauche
heresy
ignominy
libation
motley

Lesson 3
avarice
bacchanalian
bastion
copious
extradite
furtive
irascible
jettison
mercenary
ostracize

Lesson 4
appease
argot
augment
bigot
candid
chaos
expunge
jingoism
negligence
strident

Lesson 5
adamant
clement
cliché
diffident
disparity
extol
inexorable
opus
ostensible
rancor

Lesson 6
apathy
condone
connoisseur
credence
cult
dilettante
enigma
jaunty
nuance
officious

Lesson 7
ambivalent
concur
culmination
cynical
demagogue
demure
destitute
dilemma
erudite
intrepid

Lesson 8
abate
abhor
austere
decorum
dole
droll
duplicity
effigy
extrovert
gamut

Lesson 9
collaborate
contrite
emulate
enhance
enunciate
evoke
expatriate
frowzy
heinous
impeccable
impound
inane
magnanimous
sere
unctuous

Lesson 10
acrimony
balk
cajole
dour
expound
exult
feasible
fiasco
fluctuate
harry
incognito
inscrutable
lethargy
métier
omniscient

Lesson 11
affable
agrarian
arduous
avid
dolorous
epistle
explicit
formidable
gadfly
gargantuan
grandiloquent
grimace
harangue
humility
sycophant

Lesson 12
altercation
audacity
evince
exhort
expedient
galvanize
hue
hyperbole
implacable
incarcerate
incisive
lexicon
ominous
pertinent
sanction

Lesson 13
acquit
adulation
barrister
bawdy
chastise
circumvent
clandestine
culinary
deprecate
frugal
inert
jocose
latent
myriad
pernicious

Lesson 14
amicable
bask
charlatan
enraptured
fickle
genial
hoax
juggernaut
levity
marital
mundane
naive
nocturnal
novice
obstreperous

Lesson 15
befuddle
chutzpah
complacent
connive
crass
fallacy
hypercritical
indiscreet
laudable
liege
noxious
odium
pandemonium
parsimonious
verbose

Lesson 16
linguistics
pique
plebeian
precocious
predatory
prowess
pugnacious
purloin
pusillanimous
quell
quixotic
rabble
rabid
raconteur
vindictive

Lesson 17
agnostic
caustic
circumspect
exodus
hurtle
penitent
raillery
renegade
retribution
scourge
taciturn
terse
uncanny
vindicate
zephyr

Lesson 18
discordant
expedite
filibuster
impregnable
inherent
invective
irreverent
pithy
pliable
pristine
prodigal
subjugate
tenuous
torpid
xenophobia

Lesson 19
approbation
arbiter
archetype
attrition
burgeon
commensurate
confluence
coup
epicurean
mellifluous
oeuvre
secular
vacuous
vagary
verdant

Lesson 20
accolade
demur
derivative
dissident
insouciant
invidious
limpid
petulant
proliferate
ruminate
static
stipulate
tenet
vigilant
zeitgeist

Lesson 21
albeit
ancillary
asinine
august
autodidact
behest
conduit
dossier
indefatigable
indiscretion
martyr
osmosis
philatelist
picayune
semblance

Lesson One

1. **divulge** (di vulj´) *v.* to tell; to reveal (as a secret)
   The reporter was fired when she *divulged* information from a classified document.
   syn: unveil; disclose *ant: conceal*

2. **abet** (ə bet´) *v.* to assist or encourage, especially in wrongdoing
   Jim refused to *abet* the criminal by hiding him in the basement.
   syn: promote; incite *ant: impede; dissuade*

3. **dogmatic** (dôg mat´ ik) *adj.* arrogant and stubborn about one's (often unproven) beliefs
   Because of the professor's *dogmatic* approach, the students were afraid to ask questions.
   syn: dictatorial *ant: open-minded*

4. **insipid** (in sip´ id) *adj.* lacking flavor; dull; not at all stimulating
   My mom wanted me to be an accountant, but I found the classes boring and *insipid.*
   syn: flat; lifeless *ant: challenging*

5. **extraneous** (ik strā´ nē əs) *adj.* inessential; not constituting a vital part
   The professor felt that the *extraneous* paragraph in the essay detracted from the more important information.
   syn: irrelevant *ant: essential*

6. **coerce** (kō ûrs´) *v.* to force by using pressure, intimidation, or threats
   Jerry preferred basketball, but his father *coerced* him into playing football.
   syn: compel

7. **jaundiced** (jôn´ dist) *adj.* prejudiced; hostile
   Gabe had a *jaundiced* view of Iraq after losing his wife in the Gulf War.
   syn: skeptical; cynical *ant: believing; trusting*

8. **meticulous** (mi tik´ yə ləs) *adj.* extremely, sometimes excessively, careful about small details; precise
   With *meticulous* care, he crafted a miniature dollhouse for his daughter.
   syn: fastidious *ant: sloppy*

9. **temerity** (tə mer´ i tē) *n.* recklessness; a foolish disregard of danger
I couldn't believe that Bret had the *temerity* to bungee jump over a lake full of alligators.
syn: audacity *ant: prudence*

10. **gregarious** (gri gâr´ ē əs) *adj.* sociable; fond of the company of others
Just before he was diagnosed with clinical depression, Raji went from being *gregarious* to being antisocial.
syn: genial; friendly *ant: reclusive*

EXERCISE I—Words in Context

From the list below, supply the words needed to complete the paragraph. Some words will not be used.

divulge abet temerity insipid gregarious coerce jaundiced

A. Jasmine had thought that her irresponsible days of __________ were far behind her until Kayla showed up at her door. After only three days of freedom from the county correctional facility, Kayla had begun her old scheming again. She went to the house to __________ Jasmine into helping her move a truckload of stolen goods to another state—an easy job, she claimed, and virtually no risk. It would even be fun, she claimed.

"Let me get this straight. You've been out of jail for three days, and you already want me to __________ you in a crime? Are you crazy?"

Jasmine was still __________ toward her sister because Kayla, prior to her first sentence, "borrowed" Jasmine's car for a robbery and nearly got Jasmine arrested as a result.

"Sorry, Kayla, but I'm quite happy with my ___________, uneventful life. Please leave, and don't come back."

From the list below, supply the words needed to complete the paragraph. Some words will not be used.

dogmatic abet gregarious divulge extraneous coerce meticulous

B. Mr. Knight learned the __________ art of watchmaking during a three-year stay in Switzerland more than forty years ago. Since that time, he has spent countless evenings in his basement workshop assembling the tiny, complex machines. As a[n] __________ grandfather, Mr. Knight often invites his grandchildren to his shop, where they watch with amazement through a large magnifying glass and see a newly assembled pocket watch tick for the first time.

"Watches are such perfect machines; there's no room for __________ parts or over-engineering. And then, to see such a tiny machine operate under its own power—it amazes me every time."

When asked about his thoughts on the mass production techniques of modern watches, Knight revealed his __________ belief that Old World skills made watches much more valuable.

"Oh, yes, the new watches are inexpensive and readily available, which fills the practical need, but they lack the sentiment and the many hours of craftsmanship that should go into a fine piece of jewelry."

"These watches," he says as he points to a sparkling display cabinet, "have character."

Mr. Knight hopes someday to __________ the many secrets of his trade to his youngest grandson, who can then carry on the family tradition for years to come.

EXERCISE II—Sentence Completion

Complete the sentence in a way that shows you understand the meaning of the italicized vocabulary word.

1. Rhea lacks *temerity*, so she definitely would not…
2. I've never been *gregarious*, so at parties I tend to…
3. Mel thinks musicals are *insipid*, so when I asked her to see *Miss Saigon* with me, she…
4. Hikers should avoid packing *extraneous* gear because…
5. A *jaundiced* judge might not be able to…
6. Lisa decided to *abet* the bank robber by…
7. Anna's *meticulous* cleaning habits ensure that her room is always…
8. I made my psychiatrist promise not to *divulge* any…
9. My *dogmatic* English teacher refused to…
10. My boss tried to *coerce* me into attending the company picnic by…

EXERCISE III—Roots, Prefixes, and Suffixes

Study the entries and answer the questions below.

The prefix *mal* means "bad" or "evil."
The root *bene* means "good."
The root *dict* means "to speak."
The root *vol* means "to wish."
The root *fact* means "making, doing"; *factor* means "one who does."

A. Using literal translations as guidance, define the following words without using a dictionary.

1. malevolent
2. malediction
3. malefactor
4. benevolent
5. benediction
6. benefactor

B. After a biopsy, tumors are generally labeled __________ or __________.

C. List as many other related words as you can that begin with either *mal* or *bene*.

EXERCISE IV—Inference

Complete the sentences by inferring information about the italicized word from its context.

A. If students complain about a teacher's *insipid* lectures, the teacher should…

B. Since dad had a handful of *extraneous* parts after assembling Kyle's bicycle, Kyle might…

C. Martin's refusal to *divulge* the location of the military base probably means that the base is…

EXERCISE V—Writing

Here is a writing prompt similar to the one you will find on the writing portion of the SAT.

Plan and write an essay based on the following statement:

> Happiness is an imaginary condition, formerly often attributed by the living to the dead, now usually attributed by adults to children and by children to adults.
>
> – Thomas Szasz
>
> From: *The Columbia World of Quotations.* New York: Columbia University Press, 1996.

Assignment: Do you agree or disagree with Szasz's view that happiness is merely imaginary? Write an essay in which you support or refute Szasz's position. Be certain to support your point with evidence from your own reading, classroom studies, and experience.

Thesis: Write a *one-sentence* response to the above assignment. Make certain this single sentence offers a clear statement of your position.

Example: Happiness is not imaginary, but it is an elusive condition because unhappy people see only the happiness of others.

Organizational Plan: If your thesis is the point on which you want to end, where does your essay need to begin? List the points of development that are inevitable in leading your reader from your beginning point to your end point. This list is your outline.

Draft: Use your thesis as both your beginning and your end. Following your outline, write a good first draft of your essay. Remember to support all your points with examples, facts, references to reading, etc.

Review and Revise: Exchange essays with a classmate. Using the scoring guide for Organization on page 206, score your partner's essay (while he or she scores yours). Focus on the organizational plan and use of language conventions. If necessary, rewrite your essay to improve the organizational plan and the use of language.

Identifying Sentence Errors

Identify the errors in the following sentences. If the sentence contains no error, select answer E.

1. If the alarm had gone off earlier, more people could of escaped before the
   (A) had gone off (B) more people (C) could of escaped
   building collapsed. No error.
   (D) collapsed. (E) No error.

2. The principals of good sportsmanship demand that we cheer the achievements of both teams. No error.
   (A) principals of good sportsmanship (B) that we cheer (C) achievements (D) both teams (E) No error.

3. Neither Kelley nor Larry are planning to attend the conference in November. No error.
   (A) Kelley nor Larry (B) are planning (C) the conference (D) November (E) No error.

4. The boat sailed under the bridge and was rocking from the waves. No error.
   (A) The boat (B) sailed (C) under the bridge (D) was rocking from the waves (E) No error.

5. There were less people on that cruise than usual because of the weather. No error.
   (A) There were (B) less people (C) cruise (D) because of the weather (E) No error.

Improving Sentences

The underlined portion of each sentence below contains some flaw. Select the answer that best corrects the flaw.

6. Lori said to her mother that she needed to buy some new clothes.
   A. Lori said to her mother that Lori needed
   B. Lori said to her mother that her mother needed
   C. Lori's mom wanted to buy herself some new clothes
   D. Lori said that her mother needed to buy
   E. Lori said to her mother that, "She needs to buy some new clothes."

7. Softened by the boiling water, Ramona mashed the potatoes.
   A. Ramona, softened by the boiling water, mashed the potatoes.
   B. Ramona mashed the potatoes that were softened by the boiling water.
   C. Ramona mashed the softened potatoes by the boiling water.
   D. The potatoes softened by the boiling water Ramona mashed.
   E. The potatoes softened by the boiling water mashed Ramona.

8. The founders of the United States selected the colors of the flag for their symbolism: white for the purity of the new nation's aspirations, red to stand for the blood shed gaining and keeping freedom, and blue for loyalty.
   A. red, which stands for the blood,
   B. red that stands for the blood
   C. red for the blood
   D. red, the color of blood
   E. red like the blood

9. After several attempts to call, Doug still couldn't get through the line was always busy.
   A. get through, the line was
   B. get through – the line was
   C. get through although the line was
   D. get through, and the line was
   E. get through because the line was

10. Because she was on a diet, Naomi only ate three light meals a day.
    A. only Naomi ate three light meals
    B. Naomi ate only three light meals
    C. Naomi ate three light meals a day only
    D. Naomi easily ate three light meals
    E. only three light meals a day were eaten by Naomi

Lesson Two

1. **heresy** (her´ i sē) *n.* the crime of holding a belief that goes against established doctrine
   During the Inquisition, those found guilty of *heresy* were sometimes burned at the stake.
   ant: orthodoxy

2. **docile** (dos´ əl) *adj.* easy to teach or manage
   The poodle, usually *docile*, went mad and attacked its owner.
   syn: submissive; compliant *ant: unmanageable; willful*

3. **libation** (lī bā´ shən) *n.* a drink, especially an alcoholic one
   When we visited the vineyard, we were offered a small *libation* at the end of our tour.
   syn: intoxicant

4. **anathema** (ə nath´ ə mə) *n.* 1. a hated, repellant person or thing
   2. a formal curse
   1. Cannibalism is *anathema* to almost every society on the planet.
   2. The prisoner spouted anathemas at the guards as they dragged him to the gallows.
   1. *syn: abhorration; detestation* *ant: beloved*
   2. *syn: condemnation* *ant: blessing; praise*

5. **banter** (ban´ tər) *n.* teasing; playful conversation
   At the reunion, Ruth enjoyed listening to the *banter* of her husband and his old college roommate.
   syn: joshing; badinage; raillery *ant: vituperation*

6. **castigate** (kas´ ti gāt) *v.* to criticize or punish severely
   The parson *castigated* the boy for noisily chewing gum in church.
   syn: reprimand; chastise; scold *ant: praise*

7. **gauche** (gōsh) *adj.* lacking social graces; tactless
   Some people use a fork to eat pizza because they think it is *gauche* to use their fingers.
   syn: awkward *ant: graceful*

8. **ignominy** (ig´ nə min ē) *n.* public shame, disgrace, or dishonor
   The mayor fell from acclaim to *ignominy* in a week when her cocaine habit was discovered.
   syn: disgrace; infamy *ant: renown; eminence; repute*

9. **motley** (mot´ lē) *adj.* made up of dissimilar parts; being of many colors
   The international clown convention was a *motley* sight in the otherwise dull exhibition center.
   syn: varied *ant: uniform; homogeneous; similar*

10. **emaciated** (i mā´ shē āt ed) *adj.* extremely thin; wasted away
    Dead from starvation, the *emaciated* prisoner was buried in the camp cemetery.
    syn: withered *ant: plump; fattened*

EXERCISE I—Words in Context

From the list below, supply the words needed to complete the paragraph. Some words will not be used.

gauche castigate heresy banter anathema ignominy emaciated

A. After five years of starvation and torture, the __________ Kwame prayed for death. Hope was a foreign concept to him now; he no longer remembered what it was like to live in the sunlight. When he tried to remember, all he could visualize were the three years of humiliating __________ that preceded his incarceration. He couldn't even remember the faces of his wife and children anymore.

The whole thing began when Kwame's brother, a schoolteacher, wrote a letter to a nonprofit agency in the United States to appeal for educational funds. The letter was intercepted, and Sirajul's ethics agents brought the letter to Sirajul himself. The mad dictator declared that any letter that portrayed his reign in a bad light was total __________. Kwame's brother was executed, and then, to make a point, Sirajul __________ the entire family. While dictators like Sirajul were a[n] __________ to virtually anyone in the civilized world, few people had the means to stop them.

From the list below, supply the words needed to complete the paragraph. Some words will not be used.

gauche **motley** **emaciated** **libation** **banter** **docile** **heresy**

B. The actors gathered in the banquet room after the closing night of the hit play. Sounds of lighthearted __________ filled the room, and some of the more __________ performers thought nothing of picking two or more cold __________ at a time from the trays of the servers. The players were still in costumes depicting various cultures and historic eras, and arriving guests paused at the door to take in the __________ sight. The company had just completed its twentieth and final show of a successful run, and the performers were happy to relax. The spirited staff, laughing and carousing, became __________ only when the director raised her hands to quiet the room. Anticipating her words of encouragement, none of the actors suspected that she was about to announce her retirement.

EXERCISE II—Sentence Completion

Complete the sentence in a way that shows you understand the meaning of the italicized vocabulary word.

1. If Sarita tells me that her new dress is *motley*, I can assume that it is…
2. The *emaciated* girl looked as if she had not…
3. The Spanish Inquisition charged don Torino with *heresy* for allegedly…
4. A traditional *libation* at weddings and New Year's Eve parties is…
5. A supervisor might *castigate* an employee if…
6. When the teacher returned to find a *docile* class, he knew that…
7. At a wedding, it might be considered *gauche* if you…
8. One thing that is *anathema* to our society is…
9. The television evangelist faced *ignominy* when the public…
10. If someone you have a crush on engages in extended *banter* with you, you might conclude…

EXERCISE III—Roots, Prefixes, and Suffixes

Study the entries and answer the questions that follow.

The root *anthro* means "man."
The suffix *ology* means "study of."
The root *theo* means "god" or "religion."
The suffix *oid* means "having the shape of."
The root *morph* means "shape."
The prefix *a* means "not."
The suffix *cracy* means "government by."

A. Using literal translations as guidance, define the following words without using a dictionary.

1. anthropology
2. theology
3. anthropoid
4. anthropomorphic
5. atheism
6. theocracy

B. What is studied in the science of sociology?

C. List as many words as you can think of that begin with either *anthro* or *theo* or end in *ology*.

EXERCISE IV—Inference

Complete the sentences by inferring information about the italicized word from its context.

A. When offered food for the first time in weeks, the *emaciated* castaway probably…

B. If Grace complained that Jeremy was *gauche* on the dance floor, you might assume that Jeremy was…

C. A *docile* dog is probably easier to train than an aggressive dog because…

EXERCISE V—Critical Reading

Below is a reading passage followed by several multiple-choice questions similar to the ones you will encounter on the SAT. Carefully read the passage and choose the best answer to each of the questions.

H. G. Wells, author of *The Invisible Man* and *The Time Machine,* was also very interested in history. The following passage, "Primitive Thought," is adapted from Wells's *A Short History of the World.* In it, Wells speculates on the origins of human thought and religion.

1 How did it feel to be alive in the early days of the human adventure? How did men and women think and what did they think in those remote days four hundred centuries ago? Those were days long before the written record of any human impressions, and we are left almost entirely to inference and guesswork in our answers to these questions.

2 Primitive humans probably thought very much as a child thinks. They conjured up images or images presented themselves to their minds, and they acted in accordance with the emotions these pictures aroused. So a child or an uneducated person does today. Systematic thinking is apparently a comparatively late development in human experience; it has not played any great part in human life until within the last three thousand years. And even today those who really control and order their thoughts are a small minority of humankind. Most of the world still lives by imagination and passion.

3 Probably the earliest human societies were small family groups. Just as the flocks and herds of the earlier mammals arose out of families which remained together and multiplied, so probably did the earliest human tribes. But before this could happen, a certain restraint upon the primitive egotisms of the individual had to be established. The fear of the father and respect for the mother had to be extended into adult life, and the natural jealousy of the old man of the group for the younger males as they grew up had to be mitigated. Human social life grew up out of the reaction between the instinct of the young to go off by themselves as they grew up, on the one hand, and the dangers and disadvantages of separation on the other.

4 Some writers would have us believe that respect and fear of the Old Man and the emotional reaction of the primitive to older protective women, exaggerated in dreams and enriched by imagination, played a large part in the beginnings of primitive religion and in the conception of gods and goddesses. Associated with this respect for powerful or helpful personalities was a dread and exaltation of such personages after their deaths, due to their reappearance in dreams. It was easy to believe they were not truly dead but only fantastically transferred to a remoteness of greater power.

5 The dreams, imaginations, and fears of a child are far more vivid and real than those of a modern adult, and primitive humans were always somewhat like children. They were nearer to the animals also, and could suppose these animals to have motives and reactions like their own. They could imagine animal helpers, animal enemies, animal gods. One needs only to have been an imaginative child

oneself to realize again how important, significant, portentous or kind strangely shaped rocks, lumps of wood, exceptional trees, or the like may have appeared to the men of the Old Stone Age; and how dream and fancy would create stories and legends about such things that would become credible as they were told. Some of these stories would be good enough to remember and tell again. The women would tell them to the children and so establish a tradition. To this day most imaginative children invent stories in which some favourite doll or animal or some fantastic being figures as the hero, and primitive storytellers probably did the same—with a much stronger disposition to believe his hero real.

6 At the same time, primitive humans were not very critical in their associations of cause with effect; they very easily connected an effect with something quite wrong as its cause. "You do so and so," they said, "and so and so happens." You give a child a poisonous berry and it dies. You eat the heart of a valiant enemy and you become strong. There we have two bits of cause and effect association, one true one false. We call the system of cause and effect in the mind of a primitive, Fetish; but Fetish is simply primitive science. It differs from modern science in that it is totally unsystematic and uncritical and so more frequently wrong.

7 In many cases other erroneous ideas were soon corrected by experience; but there was a large series of issues of very great importance to primitive humans, where they sought persistently for causes and found explanations that were wrong but not sufficiently wrong nor so obviously wrong as to be detected. It was a matter of great importance to them that game should be abundant or fish plentiful and easily caught, and no doubt they tried and believed in a thousand charms, incantations and omens to determine these desirable results. Another great concern of his was illness and death. Occasionally infections crept through the land and people died of them. Occasionally people were stricken by illness and died or were enfeebled without any manifest cause. This too must have given the hasty, emotional primitive mind much feverish exercise. Dreams and fantastic guesses made primitive people blame this, or appeal for help to that person, or beast, or thing.

8 Quite early in the little human tribe, older, steadier minds who shared the fears and the imaginations, but who were a little more forceful than the others must have asserted themselves, to advise, to prescribe, to command. This they declared unlucky and that imperative; this an omen of good and that an omen of evil. The expert in Fetish, the Medicine Man, was the first priest. He exhorted, he interpreted dreams, he warned, he performed the complicated hocus pocus that brought luck or averted calamity. Primitive religion was not so much what we now call religion as practice and observance, and the early priest dictated what was indeed an arbitrary primitive practical science.

1. According to paragraph 2, people who think systematically
   A. determine the course of human progression.
   B. think with childlike minds.
   C. are outnumbered by people driven by emotion.
   D. composed a large portion of early civilization.
   E. are the modern equivalent of medicine men.

2. The overall tone of this passage is
   A. simplistic and speculative.
   B. scholarly and authoritative.
   C. facetious and entertaining.
   D. esoteric and thoughtful.
   E. strident and conciliatory.

3. As used in the passage, the word *egotism* (paragraph 3) most nearly means
   A. self-importance.
   B. vanity.
   C. self-consciousness.
   D. conceit.
   E. self-centeredness.

4. Which choice best states the psychological conflict that guided human social interaction?
   A. fear of father versus respect for mother
   B. dangers of separation versus desire to be independent
   C. jealousy of elders versus fear of separation
   D. instinct to be independent versus jealousy of larger families
   E. desires to remain together versus respect for father

5. As used in paragraph 5, the word *fancy* most nearly means
   A. embellished.
   B. elegant.
   C. imagination.
   D. fond.
   E. anxious.

6. Which of the following is the best paraphrase of the sentence "Fetish is simply primitive science" (paragraph 6)?
   A. Science is not based on superstition.
   B. The science of fetishism is simple and, therefore, primitive.
   C. The original word for science was fetish.
   D. The roots of modern science lie in superstition.
   E. Fetish and superstition are primitive.

7. According to paragraph 8, how did primitive Medicine Men attain their status?
   A. They demonstrated more knowledge and power than others in their tribe.
   B. They rose in status by asserting their charismatic personalities.
   C. The oldest man in the tribe was chosen as Medicine Man.
   D. The strongest warrior in the tribe was chosen as Medicine Man.
   E. The Medicine Man was revealed in a tribal dream.

8. According to the passage, which of the following is *not* a step in the development of primitive science and religion?
   A. Primitive people observed events and their apparent causes.
   B. Primitive people attempted to find the means to control the forces that affected their lives.
   C. Primitive people attributed power to other people, animals, and objects.
   D. Primitive people elected a priest from among their tribal members.
   E. Primitive people developed ritual from behavior they thought would protect them from harm.

9. According to this passage, primitive religion was the precursor to
   A. tribal belief systems.
   B. superstition.
   C. practical science.
   D. respect for elders.
   E. a rapid increase in population.

10. This passage would most likely be found in
    A. a popular science magazine.
    B. an introductory history book.
    C. an encyclopedia of world religion.
    D. a book of ancient mythology.
    E. a doctoral dissertation.

Lesson Three

1. **avarice** (av´ ə ris) *n.* greed; desire for wealth
   He became a doctor, not to save lives but to appease his *avarice.*
   syn: acquisitiveness *ant: largesse*

2. **furtive** (fûr´ tiv) *adj.* stealthy; secretive
   Not wanting to be rude, Jean cast a *furtive* glance at the man's prominent scar.
   syn: surreptitious; sneaky *ant: overt*

3. **bacchanalian** (bak ə nāl´ yən) *adj.* wild and drunken
   Adam paid for his *bacchanalian* weekend when he flunked the exam on Monday.
   ant: restrained

4. **extradite** (ek´ strə dīt) *v.* to turn over or deliver to the legal jurisdiction of another government or authority
   After two months of incarceration in Sacramento, the suspect was *extradited* to Florida.
   syn: deport

5. **copious** (kō´ pē əs) *adj.* numerous; large in quantity
   It is good to drink a *copious* amount of water before and after working out.
   syn: profuse *ant: sparse*

6. **irascible** (i ras´ ə bəl) *adj.* easily angered
   We walk on eggshells around Marty because he is so *irascible.*
   syn: irritable; ill-tempered *ant: easygoing*

7. **mercenary** (mûr´ sə ner ē) *n.* a professional soldier hired by a foreign army
   Though American by birth, the *mercenary* fought for France.
   ant: volunteer

8. **bastion** (bas´ chən) *n.* a strong defense or fort (or one likened to it)
   The United States has been called the *bastion* of democracy.
   syn: stronghold

9. **jettison** (jet´ i sən) *v.* to cast overboard; to discard
   The passengers quickly *jettisoned* the heavy cargo from the damaged plane.
   syn: deploy; throw away *ant: retain*

10. **ostracize** (os´ trə sīz) *v.* to banish; to shut out from a group or society by common consent
The strict religious community *ostracized* Eli when he married a woman of another faith.
syn: exile *ant: accept*

EXERCISE I—Words in Context

From the list below, supply the words needed to complete the paragraph. Some words will not be used.

extradite	**ostracize**	**furtive**	**avarice**
mercenary	**bacchanalian**	**bastion**	**copious**

A. Hired to combat an increase in drug trafficking, the __________ silently crawled through the fence line of the kingpin's plantation and found a good hiding place. For two days, Manco sat in the patch and observed the mansion—supposedly an impenetrable __________ in which the kingpin operated his international cartel. Manco was relieved to see that the rumors were false; the kingpin's __________ lifestyle of nightly parties would make Manco's job simple because of the excessive noise and inadequate light beyond the cocktail area. After a[n] __________ infiltration of the mansion, Manco would have an easy time arresting the kingpin, handcuffing him, sneaking him out, and then __________ him to the States, where he would face trial for a[n] __________ number of charges. The kingpin was a victim of his own __________—had he kept his illegal business small and untraceable, no one would have hired Manco to deal with him.

From the list below, supply the words needed to complete the paragraph. Some words will not be used.

bastion **jettison** **irascible** **avarice** **ostracize**

B. Isabel's __________ personality had gotten her into trouble before, but never as it did now. In reaction to her outburst during the assembly, Isabel's class __________ her. Classmates would not even sit next to Isabel, let alone speak to her. If her disruption had happened on a ship, Isabel thought, the passengers might have __________ her over the side.

EXERCISE II—Sentence Completion

Complete the sentence in a way that shows you understand the meaning of the italicized vocabulary word.

1. A criminal might be *extradited* to her home state for…
2. After a *bacchanalian* weekend, Ethan felt…
3. It is a burden to have an *irascible* supervisor because…
4. The *mercenary* received no payment and thus refused to…
5. Airplane passengers may have to *jettison* their luggage if…
6. The cliquish teens *ostracized* Raymond from their group because…
7. If I allow *avarice* to guide my career, I might choose to…
8. It doesn't take a *copious* rainfall in the desert to…
9. A church might be called a *bastion* of…
10. One might want to be especially *furtive* when…

EXERCISE III—Roots, Prefixes, and Suffixes

Study the entries and answer the questions that follow.

The root *aud* means "hear."
The root *herb* means "grass, weed."
The roots *cis* and *cide* mean "cut" or "kill."
The roots *vis* and *vid* mean "see."
The suffixes *ible* and *able* mean "able."
The prefix *in* means "into."

A. *Using literal translations as guidance, define the following words without using a dictionary:*

1. audible
2. visionary
3. herbicide
4. vista
5. auditory
6. incision

B. The root *sui* in the word "suicide" probably means __________.

C. List as many words as you can that have the roots *aud* and *vid* in them.

D. Write one example of an *incisive* comment.

E. List as many words as you can that end in *cide*.

EXERCISE IV—Inferences

Complete the sentences by inferring information about the italicized word from its context.

A. If the king's *avarice* gets out of control, he might decide to…

B. Even a little good-humored teasing might cause the *irascible* Cary to…

C. If his promised wages do not arrive before the battle, the *mercenary* will probably…

EXERCISE V—Writing

Here is a writing prompt similar to the one you will find on the writing portion of the SAT.

Plan and write an essay based on the following statement:

> One indication of good literature is that it "rings true"—that it touches upon a topic or issue that the reader can identify in his or her own life or experience. One literary selection that "rings true" for me is
> ______________________________________
> ______________________________________
> ______________________________________

Assignment: Write an essay in which you discuss the "truth" of the literature you have noted above. Be certain to support any generalities you make with specific references to the literature you are discussing and to your experience and observation.

Thesis: Write a *one-sentence* response to the above assignment. Make certain this single sentence offers a clear statement of your position.

Example: Because it shows the influence of world events on individuals, and depicts an authentic portrait of sacrificial love, Charles Dickens's A Tale of Two Cities reveals the truth about life, even though it is fiction.

Development of Ideas: If your thesis is the point on which you want to end, what facts or examples can you offer your reader to help him or her see your point? Make a *thorough* list of *specific* facts and examples. Number them in the order in which you think they should best be discussed. This list is your outline.

Draft: Use your thesis as both your beginning and your end. Following your outline, write a good first draft of your essay. Remember to support all your points with examples, facts, references to reading, etc.

Review and Revise: Exchange essays with a classmate. Using the scoring guide for Development of Ideas on page 207, score your partner's essay (while he or she scores yours). Focus on the development of ideas and use of language conventions. If necessary, rewrite your essay to incorporate more (or more relevant) support, and to improve your use of language.

Improving Paragraphs

Read the following passage and then answer the multiple-choice questions that follow. Note that the questions will require you to make decisions regarding the revision of the reading selection.

1 A book is now a common object, yet there was a time when the book was a rare and precious possession—a religious relic not available to the common person.

2 The earliest collections that we would recognize as "books" were elaborate manuscripts produced in European monasteries. To ensure that ancient knowledge would not be lost, monks made copies of the books they protected.

3 The books produced during this period were exquisitely and elaborately illuminated with beautiful lettering called calligraphy, and fantastic images of snakes, demons, and mythological creatures.

4 The most important thing about these manuscripts is that they were considered sacred objects. The monks who sat for years working on single chapters of the Bible were not reproducing books. They were making the word of God available to the world.

5 Eventually, the production of books moved from the Church to the University, and books began to lose some of their religious emphasis. University students did not have access to the books locked away in monasteries. Also, they needed access to new kinds of non-religious books that were not easily available even in the libraries of monasteries.

6 Two new kinds of institutions grew up around the universities to fulfill the demand: stationers and book copiers. These people provided paper and libraries of text books. When a student needed a text for a class, he would go to the stationers and copy it—by hand. The student could also pay a book copier to copy the book for him.

7 Then, the whole book-producing industry began to change with the arrival of the printing press. The printing press was not a single invention. It was the clever combination of many technologies that had been known for centuries.

8 The other inventions brought together to create a printing press were the machines used for hundreds of years in Europe and Asia to press oil from olives and wine from grapes; block printing that had been known in Europe since the return of Marco Polo from Asia.

9 The development of print technology created a need for other developments. Medieval manuscripts had been copied on vellum pages—a material made largely from linen. It was beautiful and durable, but far too expensive for the mass production of books. Likewise, the ink that had been used by the monks and later by university students and book copiers was expensive. Oil-based ink needed to be developed as well as a paper that could be mass-produced inexpensively, yet still be durable enough to print a book that would last.

10 Ironically, the first books printed were Bibles and religious texts; so, while the printing press may have made books more available, it did not necessarily affect the subject matter of books.

11 However, by the 16th and 17th Centuries, the Roman Catholic Church was losing much of its influence. Latin had been the primary language for the worship

of God and for the exchange of intellectual ideas, but this was changing with the Protestant Reformation. More people were learning to read, and they wanted to read things in their own language.

12 In addition, world exploration and the European colonization of Africa and the New World made people curious about faraway places. Writers and printers were only too happy to fill this demand for reading material for the curious middle classes. The modern book was born.

13 So the book on the shelf of a typical city library has a long and interesting ancestry that goes at least as far back as the monks in their medieval monasteries. Were it not for such different endeavors as wine-making and world travel, the book as we know it might never have been developed.

1. Which of the following revisions best clarifies the intent of paragraph 4?
   A. ...sacred objects because the monks...
   B. ...sacred objects, and the monks...
   C. ...sacred objects the monks...
   D. ...sacred objects, the monks...
   E. ...sacred objects; the monks...

2. Which of the following suggestions best corrects the awkward paragraph structure at the beginning of this selection?
   A. Add more material about the European monasteries.
   B. Delete paragraphs 2 and 3.
   C. Delete paragraphs 2 and 4.
   D. Combine paragraphs 2 and 3.
   E. Combine paragraphs 2 and 4.

3. What two paragraphs could be combined to make the passage easier to read?
   A. Paragraphs 5 and 6
   B. Paragraphs 7 and 8
   C. Paragraphs 10 and 11
   D. Paragraphs 10 and 12
   E. Paragraphs 11 and 13

4. Which of the following revisions offers a better transition between paragraphs 6 and 7?
   A. Replace the first sentence of paragraph 7 with the sentence, "The tedium of hand-copying books was soon alleviated by the arrival of the printing press."
   B. "On the other hand, the whole book-producing industry began to change…"
   C. Replace "Then" in the first sentence of paragraph 7 with "However."
   D. Use a semicolon to combine the last sentence of paragraph 6 with the first sentence of paragraph 7.
   E. Omit "Then."

5. If the passage had to be shortened, what could be omitted without changing the intent of the passage?
   A. Paragraphs 1 and 2
   B. Paragraphs 5 and 6
   C. Paragraphs 8 and 9
   D. Paragraphs 10 and 11
   E. Paragraphs 11 and 12

Lesson Four

1. **bigot** (big´ ət) *n.* one who is intolerant of differences in others
The *bigot* refused to share a cab with anyone of a different race.
syn: racist; extremist

2. **expunge** (ik spunj´) *v.* to erase or eliminate
If Moni can stay out of trouble for one year, her criminal record will be *expunged.*
syn: obliterate *ant: add*

3. **candid** (kan´ did) *adj.* outspoken; blunt
He gave a *candid* speech about the time he had spent in prison.
syn: frank; direct *ant: evasive*

4. **argot** (är´ gō) *n.* special words or phrases used by a specific group of people
Don't agree to "a trip to the East River" proposed by anyone speaking Mafia *argot.*
syn: jargon

5. **negligence** (neg´ li jəns) *n.* careless neglect, often resulting in injury
Sara's *negligence* allowed her toddler to fall from the hotel balcony.
syn: carelessness *ant: care; attention*

6. **appease** (ə pēz´) *v.* to calm; to make satisfied (often only temporarily)
The small snack before dinner did nothing to *appease* Shane's appetite.
syn: mollify *ant: aggravate*

7. **strident** (strīd´ nt) *adj.* harsh sounding; grating
Lisa's *strident* voice gave us all headaches.
syn: shrill *ant: soothing*

8. **chaos** (kā´ os) *n.* complete disorder
The new teacher was expected to end the *chaos* and restore order in the classroom.
syn: confusion; jumble *ant: order; harmony*

9. **augment** (ôg ment´) *v.* to enlarge; to increase in amount or intensity
I had to take a second job to *augment* my income after buying the new SUV.
syn: expand; supplement *ant: narrow; reduce*

10. **jingoism** (jing´ gō iz əm) *n.* extreme, chauvinistic patriotism, often favoring an aggressive, warlike foreign policy
Because of his *jingoism*, the candidate lost the support of voters.

EXERCISE I—Words in Context

From the list below, supply the words needed to complete the paragraph. Some words will not be used.

augment **jingoism** **argot** **candid** **chaos** **appease**

A. The Prime Minister faced a tough decision to __________ an angered nation. The __________ resulting from the surprise attack fueled widespread __________, and citizens were tired of the administration's inaction. When he finally spoke, the Prime Minister delivered a[n] __________ address that revealed his anger and his plan of counterattack.

From the list below, supply the words needed to complete the paragraph. Some words will not be used.

negligence	**augment**	**expunge**	**bigot**
argot	**strident**	**chaos**	**tradition**

B. Much to everyone's dislike, the outspoken __________ used the __________ of the slave trade to __________ his racial supremacy speeches. The speeches often accompanied the __________ sounds of screaming protesters, many of whom claimed that the speaker's __________ in teaching tolerance inspired his followers to commit hate crimes throughout the country. He stood alone on the stage as he addressed the angered crowd; even his former friends and colleagues wanted to __________ him from their lives.

EXERCISE II—Sentence Completion

Complete the sentence in a way that shows you understand the meaning of the italicized vocabulary word.

1. Theresa was *candid* about my new haircut; she told me that…

2. When I babysat the Patelli twins, my *negligence* led to…

3. I thought it was fair to accuse George of *jingoism* after he…

4. If I wanted to *augment* my savings account, I might…

5. The *argot* of pirates might include terms such as…

6. I realized my grandfather was a *bigot* when he told me…

7. One way to *appease* a crying child is…

8. My brother's voice becomes *strident* when he…

9. The atmosphere on the commuter train became one of *chaos* when…

10. My math teacher said he would *expunge* the "F" from my record if I…

EXERCISE III—Roots, Prefixes, and Suffixes

Study the entries and answer the questions that follow.

The root *alter* means "change" or "other."
The root *ego* means "self."
The root *mega* means "large."
The root *polis* means "city" or "state."
The root *centris* means "centered on."

A. *Using literal translations as guidance, define the following words without using a dictionary:*

1. megalopolis
2. alteration
3. alter ego
4. metropolitan
5. egotist
6. egocentric

B. A person who is a megalomaniac might not feel right unless ______________________.

C. If you alter your plans, you ______________________________.

D. List as many words as you can think of that begin with the root *ego*, and then do the same for the root *mega*.

EXERCISE IV—Inference

Complete the sentences by inferring information about the italicized word from its context.

A. The writer took offense at Marty's *candid* review because it…

B. When *negligence* becomes the main reason for damaged goods and low profits, the plant managers will probably…

C. If Colleen made *strident* sounds while practicing her saxophone, her parents probably…

EXERCISE V—Critical Reading

Below is a pair of reading passages followed by several multiple-choice questions similar to the ones you will encounter on the SAT. Carefully read the passages and choose the best answer to each of the questions.

The following pair of passages presents two accounts of a tragic incident that occurred in the coal mine region of Pennsylvania. The author of Passage 1 deals essentially with the event of the fire and the personal loss that resulted. The author of Passage 2 suggests that perhaps there was more involved than a mere accident.

Passage 1

All the small towns in the coal-rich hills of Central Pennsylvania look pretty much alike, except for Centralia. With a population of 46, Centralia is very nearly a twenty-first century ghost town.

In the early 1960's, Centralia was a prosperous town of 1,100 resi-
5 dents. People were friendly, and neighbors watched out for one another; however, all that changed in 1962 when the town selected an exhausted strip mine just outside of town as the site of a new landfill. In May of that year, a fire broke out at the dump and proved to be difficult to extinguish. Not long after the landfill fire, it was discovered that a seam
10 of coal beneath the landfill—a seam of coal that ran in an intricate web beneath the town itself—had caught fire.

That was over 40 years ago, and the fire still burns today. Sulfurous smoke vents through cracks in the pavement. Houses have collapsed into sink holes caused by mine subsidence, and the number of residents
15 has dwindled from 1,100 to 46.

In 1984, after repeated and expensive attempts by state and federal agencies to extinguish or contain the fire, the federal government finally allocated $42 million to purchase the homes and businesses of affected residents and allow them to relocate. Since then, efforts have continued
20 to remove residents from harm and close this sad story of human error and inevitable consequences.

Passage 2

On April 1, 1996—April Fools' Day—the United States Supreme Court denied an appeal of the few remaining residents of Centralia, Pennsylvania, who had filed preliminary legal objections to the condemnation of their homes. With this denial, these hapless citizens essentially
5 lost the right to their homes.

Residents who chose to stay beyond the December 31, 1997, relocation deadline would forfeit the right to compensation from any federal or state agency or any private enterprise for losses suffered, including loss of life.

10 The issue at hand was a 34-year-old mine fire burning beneath the homes, businesses, and streets of Centralia. What seemed to be an unfortunate accident in May of 1962 now appears to some to be a

conspiracy on the part of the United States government to seize the rich coal deposits that lie beneath the town and surrounding areas.
15 Proponents of the conspiracy theory cite the following facts:

- All holes in an abandoned strip mine that would have given a surface fire access to underground coal were allegedly sealed before the mine was approved for use as a landfill.
- The Commonwealth of Pennsylvania inspected the sealed holes and
20 certified the mine as safe to use.
- A few days after a May 1962 trash fire, firefighters found one hole that had been unintentionally left open. It was through this hole that the trash fire spread underground.
- Department of Natural Resources personnel drilled boreholes
25 around the site of the fire to monitor the fire's spread and the underground temperature. Some residents believe that these boreholes actually contributed to the spread of the fire by providing oxygen, without which the fire might have burnt itself out.
30 • The first—and only—serious attempt to control the burn occurred in 1969 over a holiday weekend. A trench was dug to halt the spread of the fire; however, crews worked only one shift a day and stopped for the holiday. By the time work resumed, the fire had already spread beyond the trench. Had
35 crews worked three shifts a day and not stopped for the holiday, the fire would have been contained and probably extinguished.
- Since the extinguishing effort, the only action taken by the federal government has been to buy up the homes and businesses in
40 Centralia and relocate the residents.
- In 1992, the Commonwealth of Pennsylvania was authorized by the United States Office of Surface Mining to condemn the properties of the remaining residents, who had thus far refused to accept any of the government's relocation offers.
45 • All attempts by the residents of Centralia and the Commonwealth of Pennsylvania to bring legal action to protect their rights and their homes, and the valuable coal beneath the town, have been denied.
- The April 1, 1996, Supreme Court denial ended all possibility of
50 legal action on the part of the residents and the Commonwealth of Pennsylvania.

Many remaining and former residents assert that when the final person leaves Centralia, the land and the coal will become the property of
55 the United States government. They suspect that when the government owns the land, the means of extinguishing the decades-old fire will be discovered, and the coal will be mined.

Government conspiracy or tragic accident? Perhaps only the future will tell, but for those whose entire family histories have been
60 lost, it's been a true nightmare—a sad, sad story that hasn't yet ended.

1. The overall tone of the first passage can best be described as
   A. sympathetic.
   B. apathetic.
   C. ironic.
   D. condemning.
   E. fatalistic.

2. What idea does the author of Passage 1 hope to establish in the first two sentences of the second paragraph (lines 4-7)?
   A. Life was hard in Centralia, Pennsylvania, even before the fire.
   B. Prior to the fire, Centralia, Pennsylvania, was a thriving metropolis.
   C. The early 1960s were a period of vast change for all the United States.
   D. Centralia, Pennsylvania, was a typical small town before the fire.
   E. Centralia, Pennsylvania, was an inappropriate place for a landfill.

3. As used in Passage 1 (line 14), the word *subsidence* most nearly means
   A. depletion.
   B. relocation.
   C. condemning.
   D. replenishment.
   E. erosion.

4. The phrase "repeated and expensive attempts" (line 16) implies that
   A. everything possible was done to extinguish or contain the fire.
   B. the fire has cost the residents a great deal of money.
   C. the government's attempts to extinguish or contain the fire all met with failure.
   D. new advances in firefighting technology make a solution imminently probable.
   E. the cost of extinguishing the fire greatly exceeded the cost of replacing damaged buildings.

5. The overall tone of the second passage can best be described as
   A. bitterly ironic.
   B. thoughtfully condemning.
   C. blandly objective.
   D. mildly reproachful.
   E. severely critical.

6. The purpose of the reference to April Fools' Day in the first sentence of the second passage is most likely to
   A. establish the exact date of the Supreme Court's decision.
   B. emphasize the perseverance of the residents of Centralia.
   C. imply that the Supreme Court's decision was foolish.
   D. highlight the irony that the Supreme Court's decision was handed down in spring.
   E. reinforce the importance of the issue to the residents of Centralia.

7. In Passage 2, which of the following is *not* a factor in the suspected conspiracy?
   A. The Commonwealth of Pennsylvania inspected the strip mine and certified it for use as a landfill.
   B. Boreholes drilled by the Department of Natural Resources may have provided oxygen and allowed the fire to spread.
   C. Workers worked too slowly on the containment ditch.
   D. Residents of Centralia have been denied legal appeals to the condemnation of their homes.
   E. The Supreme Court denial was handed down on April Fool's Day.

8. What does the author of Passage 2 finally conclude about the likelihood that the Centralia mine fire is a government conspiracy?
   A. The author comes to no absolute conclusion, citing only what residents claim.
   B. The author sums up the facts of the case and suggests that a conspiracy is possible.
   C. The author sums up the facts of the case and suggests that a conspiracy is not likely.
   D. The author presents the government's case clearly and succinctly to demonstrate the unlikelihood of a conspiracy.
   E. The author offers no conclusion regarding the conspiracy, but expresses sympathy for the affected residents.

9. The primary difference between the two passages is that
   A. they present two opposing views of the same issue.
   B. Passage 1 reports on the situation, while Passage 2 analyzes the situation.
   C. Passage 2 uses facts to establish a thesis, while Passage 1 merely offers vague generalities.
   D. each passage blames a different party for the fire.
   E. each passage contradicts the other on key facts.

10. Which of the following statements most accurately describes the relationship or differences between the two passages?
   A. Passage 2 is an expanded version of Passage 1.
   B. Passage 2 presents more specific information for the reader to arrive at his or her own conclusion.
   C. Passage 1 presents a more objective account of the issue.
   D. The two passages are most likely parts of a larger essay on Centralia.
   E. The information in the passages suggests that they were written by rival authors.

Lesson Five

1. **rancor** (rang´ kər) *n.* extreme hatred or ill will
   Whelan's double-dealing had Jack seething; he had never before felt so much *rancor* toward a lawyer.
   syn: animosity; enmity *ant: amity; sympathy*

2. **inexorable** (in ek´ sər ə bal) *adj.* unrelenting; unavoidable
   Decades of harsh weather caused the *inexorable* erosion of the tombstone.
   syn: relentless; certain *ant: avoidable; preventable*

3. **extol** (ik stōl´) *v.* to praise highly
   Emily *extolled* the virtues of her personal hero and mentor.
   syn: exalt; laud *ant: chastise*

4. **clement** (klem´ ənt) *adj.* merciful; lenient
   Despite the abhorrent nature of the crime, the judge handed down a surprisingly *clement* sentence.
   syn: forbearing; benign *ant: malevolent; harsh*

5. **cliché** (klē shā´) *n.* a worn-out idea or overused expression
   The candidate promised new ideas, but spouted the same old *clichés* after her election.
   syn: platitude; banality

6. **adamant** (ad´ ə mant) *adj.* unyielding; firm in opinion
   Despite the protests of the entire city council, the mayor remained *adamant.*
   syn: stubborn *ant: amenable; flexible*

7. **diffident** (dif´ i dənt) *adj.* lacking in self-confidence; shy
   The *diffident* student hated to speak in front of the class.
   syn: timid *ant: outgoing*

8. **opus** (ō´ pəs) *n.* a creative work, especially a numbered composition ("opus 3" would be a composer's third composition; plural: *opera*)
   My favorite composition by Antonin Dvorák is *Opus* 95.

9. **ostensible** (o sten´ sə bəl) *adj.* professed but not necessarily true
   The *ostensible* reason for inviting her up to his room was to show her his bottle cap collection.
   syn: supposed *ant: actual*

10. **disparity** (di spar´ i tē) *n.* inequality; difference
    My wife is twelve years older than I am, but we get along well despite the *disparity* in our ages.
    syn: gap *ant: similarity*

EXERCISE I—Words in Context

From the list below, supply the words needed to complete the paragraph. Some words will not be used.

cliché	**extol**	**adamant**	**rancor**
ostensible	**clement**	**disparity**	

A. I wish that I could __________ your recent work, but as the __________ goes, workers like you are a dime a dozen. I've been __________ by keeping you on the payroll despite your recent incompetence, but it must end now. The president is __________ about cutting unnecessary costs, so I'm afraid that I'm going to have to let you go.

From the list below, supply the words needed to complete the paragraph. Some words will not be used.

inexorable	**disparity**	**opus**	**diffident**
ostensible	**clement**	**rancor**	

B. When the manager noticed the __________ between the amount of cash in the register and the total of the nightly bank deposit, he never suspected Yvonne. __________ and mild mannered, she nonetheless was a criminal with utmost __________ for the law. Stealing had been a[n] __________ part of her life for as long as she could remember, and she had no plans to correct her habits. She had the __________ belief that her crimes were works of art, and her latest __________ required a handful of stolen cash from her job at the restaurant.

EXERCISE II—Sentence Completion

Complete the sentence in a way that shows you understand the meaning of the italicized vocabulary word.

1. Devon's *rancor* toward housework became obvious when his guests…

2. The *cliché*, "to tie the knot," actually means…

3. Aunt Rita's *adamant* belief in superstition causes her to…

4. A *diffident* person will probably never become…

5. The composer's latest *opus* will be played by…

6. Carol's *ostensible* purpose was charity, but she really wanted…

7. The *disparity* among our political opinions sometimes results in…

8. The *clement* jury found the defendant to be…

9. The Speedy-Mart manager *extolled* Jeremy for…

10. The advance of the invading forces seemed *inexorable* until…

EXERCISE III—Roots, Prefixes, and Suffixes

Study the entries and answer the questions that follow.

The prefix *circum* means "around, on all sides."
The root *naviga* means "to sail, to steer."
The prefixes *intro* and *intra* mean "in, within, inside of."
The roots *spec* and *spect* mean "to see, look at."
The roots *vert* and *vers* mean "to turn."
The root *locu* means "speaking."
The prefix *extro* means "outside."

A. *Using literal translations as guidance, define the following words without using a dictionary:*

1. circumnavigate
2. retrospect
3. introvert
4. introspect
5. circumlocutions
6. extrovert

B. List as many words as you can think of that contain the root *spec* and the root *vert*. Try to define each word literally.

C. List as many words as you can think of that contain the prefix *circum* and the prefix *intro*. Try to define each word literally.

EXERCISE IV—Inference

Complete the sentences by inferring information about the italicized word from its context.

A. Because Shelly is so *adamant* about not accepting birthday gifts, her friends could…

B. The judge was *clement* when she sentenced the offender, so the crime was probably…

C. Sierra produced twice as many widgets as needed, so her supervisor *extolled* her by…

EXERCISE V—Writing

Here is a writing prompt similar to the one you will find on the writing portion of the SAT.

Plan and write an essay based on the following statement:

> I'm always amazed that people will actually choose to sit in front of the television and just be savaged by stuff that belittles their intelligence.
>
> – Alice Walker

Assignment: Write an essay in which you interpret the above statement, and describe whether you agree or disagree. Be certain to support and illustrate your points with specific references to your experiences and observations.

Thesis: Write a *one-sentence* response to the above assignment. Make certain this single sentence offers a clear statement of your position.

Example: Though Alice Walker may believe that everything on television insults human intelligence, I find many programs to be educational and inspirational.

Organizational Plan: If your thesis is the point on which you want to end, where does your essay need to begin? List the points of development that are inevitable in leading your reader from your beginning point to your end point. This list is your outline.

Draft: Use your thesis as both your beginning and your end. Following your outline, write a good first draft of your essay. Remember to support all your points with examples, facts, references to reading, etc.

Review and Revise: Exchange essays with a classmate. Using the scoring guide for Sentence Formation and Variety on page 208, score your partner's essay (while he or she scores yours). Focus on sentence structure and use of language conventions. If necessary, rewrite your essay to improve the sentence structure and the use of language.

Identifying Sentence Errors

Identify the errors in the following sentences. If the sentence contains no error, select answer E.

1. Many people go to the movies to escape reality, but my best friend and me go to be entertained. No error.
   (A) Many people (B) to escape reality (C) my best friend and me (D) to be entertained (E) No error

2. Everyone should have a dream that they can strive for, even if it sometimes seems impossible to achieve it. No error.
   (A) should have (B) they can (C) even if (D) seems (E) No error

3. If Deanna or Katie win the election for class president, I'll be disappointed. No error.
   (A) If (B) win (C) for class president (D) I'll be disappointed (E) No error

4. I laughed when I saw my neighbor, Mr. Bean, yelling at people in the street in his long underwear. No error.
   (A) I laughed (B) my neighbor, Mr. Bean (C) yelling at people in the street (D) in his long underwear (E) No error

5. During the holidays, my family and I traveled further than we did last year. No error.
   (A) During the holidays (B) family and I (C) traveled further (D) we did (E) No error

Improving Sentences

The underlined portion of each sentence below contains some flaw. Select the answer that best corrects the flaw.

6. Because I relied on my calculator so often, I had forgotten how to do long division.
   A. I forgot how to do long division.
   B. I have forgotten how long division works.
   C. I forget how to do long division.
   D. long division had become impossible.
   E. long division became a mystery.

7. My parents trusted me with their new car because I passed the driving test without a problem, I studied for it for more than a month.
   A. My parents trusted me with their new car because I passed the driving test without a problem, but I spent more than a month studying for it.
   B. My parents trusted me with their new car because I passed the driving test without a problem, and I studied for it for more than a month.
   C. My parents trusted me with their new car because I passed the driving test without a problem, even though I had studied for it for more than a month.
   D. My parents, who trusted me with their new car because I passed the driving test without a problem, and studied for it for more than a month.
   E. My parents trusted me with their new car, because I passed the driving test without a problem, yet studied for it for more than a month.

8. In the United States, we can vote and will be able to sign contracts legally at the age of 18.
   A. we can vote and then sign contracts…
   B. we vote and can sign contracts…
   C. we can vote and sign contracts…
   D. we can vote and are permitted to sign contracts…
   E. we can vote and are able to sign contracts…

9. Do the people who use cell phones driving cause more accidents than are caused by others?
   A. Do the people on cell phones while driving cause more accidents than are caused by others?
   B. Do the people who use cell phones while they are driving cause more accidents than other people will do?
   C. Do the people who use cell phones driving cause more accidents than others?
   D. Do the people who use cell phones while driving cause more accidents than people who don't?
   E. Do the people who use cell phones driving cause more accidents than those who don't use cell phones in the car?

10. Natalie raised her voice above the loud music to be heard.
   A. above the loud music, so people would be able to hear her.
   B. to be heard above the loud music.
   C. above the loud music so her words could be heard.
   D. over the noise to be heard.
   E. so that she would be able to be clearly heard over the very loud music.

Lesson Six

1. **condone** (kən dōn´) *v.* to forgive or overlook an offense
After hearing about the man's starving family, most found it easy to *condone* his theft of the food.
syn: pardon; excuse *ant: condemn*

2. **nuance** (nōō´ äns) *n.* a slight or subtle degree of difference
The sharpest listeners detected a *nuance* in the speaker's tone that revealed her opinion.
syn: gradation; shade

3. **connoisseur** (kon ə sûr´) *n.* an expert in matters of culture, food, or wine
The chef watched nervously as the *connoisseur* tasted the soup.
ant: tyro; novice; neophyte

4. **enigma** (i nig´ mə) *n.* a mystery; something seemingly inexplicable
Mona Lisa's smile is an *enigma* because no one knows the thoughts behind her inscrutable expression.
syn: riddle; puzzle

5. **apathy** (ap´ ə thē) *n.* lack of interest; state of not caring
The fund drive to raise money for a new gym failed because of student *apathy*.
syn: indifference *ant: interest; eagerness*

6. **officious** (ə fĭsh´ əs) *adj.* excessively eager to deliver unasked-for or unwanted help
I wish my *officious* sister would stop telling me how to run my life.
syn: meddlesome; interfering

7. **credence** (krēd´ ns) *n.* belief or trust
Surprisingly, Shayna's teacher gave *credence* to her story about how she lost her homework.
syn: faith; confidence *ant: disbelief*

8. **jaunty** (jôn´ tē) *adj.* having a buoyant, self-confident air; brisk and crisp
My three-year-old always walks in a *jaunty* manner when I put him in that sailor suit.
syn: confident; poised

9. **dilettante** (dil i tänt´) *n.* one who merely dabbles in an art or a science
The *dilettante* felt that his superficial knowledge of art qualified him to judge the artist's work.
syn: amateur; trifler *ant: expert; professional*

10. **cult** (kult) *n.* an organized group of people with an obsessive devotion to a person or set of principles
To join the *cult*, recruits had to shave their heads and walk over burning coals.
syn: sect

EXERCISE I—Words in Context

From the list below, supply the words needed to complete the paragraph. Some words will not be used.

condone	**nuance**	**connoisseur**	**apathy**
officious	**cult**	**credence**	**dilettante**

A. The chef, tucked away in the kitchen, nervously awaited the report from the latest critic. Knowing that Mr. Tahoma was a[n] __________ of Peruvian cuisine and a weekly newspaper columnist with a[n] __________ following, the chef hoped that the waiters refrained from the __________ behavior that well-known food critics must often endure from servers. The chef had run the restaurant for twenty-eight years; he was certainly not a[n] __________ in matters of cooking, but owing to a decline in customers, he worried about the fate of the business. He could only hope that Mr. Tahoma would rave about the many subtle __________ of flavor in the meal. A positive review, combined with the __________ accorded to the column, might be all that the chef needed to save the restaurant.

From the list below, supply the words needed to complete the paragraph. Some words will not be used.

credence **condone** **nuance** **enigma** **apathy** **jaunty**

B. Though she was a hostess at the restaurant, Rolinda remained seated even as customers entered the waiting area. Quietly expressing her __________ about hungry suburbanites, Rolinda confined herself to a sigh and let younger servers greet the new potential tippers at the door. She knew that no manager could be expected to __________ such behavior. Rolinda also wondered why, even though she hadn't been sick, she had been so tired for the last month. If she didn't solve this __________ soon, she would more than likely lose her job. For another day, she would just have to put on a fake smile and affect a[n] __________ manner until the end of her shift.

EXERCISE II—Sentence Completion

Complete the sentence in a way that shows you understand the meaning of the italicized vocabulary word.

1. Parents cannot *condone* their children's actions when…

2. The *dilettante* never grew tired of watching the stars, hoping someday to…

3. "This case is quite an *enigma*," said the detective. We'll be lucky to…

4. To show their loyalty, members of the *cult* wear…

5. The *connoisseur* was world-reknowned for her ability to identify the tastes of specific…

6. Giving *credence* to the refugees' story, the border guard…

7. Never voting or reading the newspaper revealed Kenton's *apathy* for…

8. After enduring her *officious* mother for more than thirty years, Loren decided to…

9. Nick had a *jaunty* walk after winning…

10. The extra seasoning in the recipe gave the chicken a *nuance* of…

EXERCISE III—Roots, Prefixes, and Suffixes

Study the entries and answer the questions that follow.

The root *arch* means "rule," "govern," or "to be first."
The roots *dem* and *demos* mean "people."
The roots *mit* and *mis* mean "send."
The suffix *ist* means "one who practices or believes."
The suffix *cracy* means "rule by."
The suffix *graphy* means "writing about" or "study of."

A. Using literal translations as guidance, define the following words without using a dictionary.

1. archetype
2. transmit
3. democracy
4. demography
5. monarchy
6. remit

B. A technocrat would be a supporter of ______________________.

C. The root *oligos* means few; therefore, an oligarchy would probably be ______________________.

D. List as many words as you can think of that contain the forms *arch, dem, mit, mis, or crat.*

E. The prefix *an* means "without" or "against." An anarchist is ______________________.

EXERCISE IV—Inference

Complete the sentences by inferring information about the italicized word from its context.

A. The *connoisseur* refused a considerable sum to endorse the fast-food chain because she believed that…

B. When the *apathy* of your coworkers causes them to ignore your requests, the best way to get their attention is to…

C. The case of the stolen emeralds remains an *enigma*, so the detective will probably…

EXERCISE V—Critical Reading

Below is a reading passage followed by several multiple-choice questions similar to the ones you will encounter on the SAT. Carefully read the passage and choose the best answer for each of the questions.

The author of the following passage offers a view on aging that is considerably different from the view espoused by popular culture, focusing on the benefits of aging rather than the disadvantages.

1 We are told that by the year 2030, one of every four Americans will be at least 60 years of age, so one benefit of advancing age will be having lots of company. A secondary benefit is knowing that tasks we took on as young adults are completed, and we can enjoy our years of relaxation.

2 Our bodies have been changing throughout our lives, and growth and change have been continuous parts of maturation. As infants, we experienced a change in eye color, bone strength, tooth formation, size, and weight almost every day. Going from one stage to another is nothing new to us, but in our early growing years we were so busy waiting to be 13, 16, 18, and 21 that we were not paying much attention to slight differences in our physical makeup. What changes we were aware of, such as height and physical strength, were often welcomed.

3 Adapting to any stage of life is common to us all, even if the changes we encounter are those found in aging. Aging is as normal as an infant's learning to walk and talk, and once accepted, no more difficult to get used to. As we all speak differently, so will each of us change differently with age, and our adaptations to life as we advance will evoke as many different reactions.

4 Nothing really changes as far as basic needs are concerned. We will always need air, food, water, clothing, shelter, and sometimes medical care. Our handling of all these needs may change over the years as we find ourselves providing for someone else, and eventually, having someone else provide for us.

5 Limitations in sight, hearing, and mobility may herald our continuing progression through life's stages, but as long as we are aware that there are ways of coping with every situation, we need not be apprehensive.

6 People are inherently independent and have a tendency toward self-sufficiency that perseveres no matter the age. Our needs for companionship and a feeling of self-worth never diminish, because we all want to be a productive part of our world community—to see a purpose for our lives. None of us desires uselessness, and we want to feel that we will never cease to have a place in the society to which we have already made many contributions.

7 Remaining mentally alert and maintaining a high level of emotional health are paramount in adjusting to advancing age. Being socially active is an important first step in the process, and volunteerism is a good way to achieve it. Sharing experiences with those who may benefit from hearing them and offering aid to worthy causes help us to maintain a positive outlook and self-image.

8 Physical limitations or even total confinement need not hamper social involvement. Mental activities such as reading and keeping a journal are productive exercises that can be accomplished in one's own home. Interpersonal relationships can provide strong support but do not necessitate traveling away from home. The telephone has long been the device used for people to "reach out and touch someone"; similarly, the computer and the Internet now offer nearly everyone the ability to keep in touch through e-mail and instant messaging technology. Restrictive physical changes should be looked at as challenges rather than hindrances and may actually bring about the learning of new practices, arts, crafts, and outward expressions of personality or hidden talents.

9 As senescence brings about changes in hearing or vision, we find these differences can be endured more readily than drastic changes in movement such as those brought on by stroke or serious accident. For hearing or vision loss, occupational therapists can make us aware of devices we can learn to rely on, or ways of enhancing remaining capabilities by placing positive importance on substituting one sense for another. Taste and smell, for example, can be dependable supportive senses when vision diminishes, and touch and sight can compensate for hearing loss. Eyeglasses and hearing aids may become part of everyday attire with relative ease; however, improvements to loss of mobility may be considerably more challenging.

10 Occupational therapists can assist in regaining full or partial freedom of movement after a period of inactivity following stroke or accident. These therapists are specially trained experts who can help a person adapt to each physical challenge in ways that defy constraints of demanding situations at home or away. They can help us find new capabilities and adjust our attitudes by encouraging the natural instinct for self-sufficiency and independence. Their vast knowledge of many types of equipment, such as chair elevators, mobile carts, walkers, wheelchairs, canes, and the use of heat and massage, is extremely valuable reinforcement.

11 Health professionals can also lead us to make correct decisions about our care if memory loss occurs. They help us to determine whether a physical change is responsible for memory problems or whether further medical attention should be sought when conditions that are more serious are suspected.

12 The most important thing to keep in mind is that there are many more resources available than ever before. Aging is no longer something to be dreaded. We have access to a great deal of help from many different agencies and support groups, with more sources emerging every day. Coping with changes in life has never been easy, but with so many shoulders to share the burdens, the most difficult thing we may have to do is ask for help.

1. The intention of this passage is to
   A. remind us that we will all be growing old.
   B. inform young people that they will have certain maladies later in life.
   C. tell people what type of professionals they must call when aging.
   D. reassure people that aging is not a condition to be feared.
   E. offer suggestions for what older people can do while waiting to die.

2. In the beginning of the passage, what is meant by the statement, "Going from one stage to another is nothing new to us…"?
   A. We changed from being babies to being children, to being teens, to being adults.
   B. We are accustomed to changing our addresses, our clothes, our cars, our furniture.
   C. We can live with changes in our own lives because we have seen changes in others.
   D. We have gone from one era to another like human beings all over the world.
   E. We are not strangers to seeing different ages, such as the ice age, the iron age, the atomic age, etc.

3. By emphasizing that adaptation is a common human trait, paragraph 3 is attempting
   A. to show that babies learn to walk, and so does everyone else.
   B. to show that all of us speak the same language, but with different accents.
   C. to show that there is nothing abnormal or unduly difficult in facing changes associated with aging.
   D. to show that growing old is just like learning to talk and walk for the first time.
   E. to prove that infants learn to talk in the same way as older people.

4. What is the purpose of telling us our basic needs if they remain the same (paragraph 4)?
   A. Medical care should be added to what we know are basic needs.
   B. We need to be reminded that we require all the things mentioned.
   C. We need to be told we cannot survive without air, water, food, etc.
   D. A checklist can be formed using the guidelines set forth in the passage.
   E. Basic needs do not change, but our use of them does.

5. In paragraph 6, what is meant by "self-sufficiency that perseveres no matter the age?"
    A. Self-sufficiency is something we all want, no matter which era we live in.
    B. No matter how old we are, we still want to be able to take care of ourselves.
    C. No matter how we age, we are still sufficiently aware of ourselves.
    D. Being old doesn't mean that we can still take care of ourselves sufficiently.
    E. We persevere sufficiently no matter how old we get.

6. The word "paramount" in paragraph 7 is used to express
    A. that movie theaters keep us mentally alert.
    B. the highest level of our activity is mental.
    C. that mental and emotional health are the same thing.
    D. only people with self-esteem are mentally alert.
    E. the importance of mental and emotional health.

7. The main idea of paragraph 8 is
    A. to remind us that only old people can stay at home because of physical impairment.
    B. that we shouldn't stay at home just because we get old.
    C. to show that physical impairment can lead to discovery of other capabilities.
    D. to show that we all need friends, especially at home.
    E. that being a total shut-in is not so bad if you have some friends.

8. Given the context of the passage, the word *senescence* most nearly means
    A. a lack of interest in reading.
    B. deteriorating physical abilities.
    C. the inability to see and hear.
    D. the process of aging.
    E. the loss of balance following a stroke or accident.

9. What is the main purpose of the last two paragraphs?
    A. They give final advice about aging and how to seek help.
    B. They conclude the passage with a summary of information.
    C. They lead the reader to want to make notes about the passage.
    D. They ask the reader to call someone.
    E. They offer a few final words of encouragement.

10. An appropriate title for the entire passage might be
    A. Being old doesn't mean having a second childhood.
    B. We can live with aging; it's just another stage of life.
    C. Help for the elderly is on the way, and we can get it.
    D. Aging is beneficial once you get used to it.
    E. Aging is the concern of everyone—young and old.

Lesson Seven

1. **cynical** (sin´ i kəl) *adj.* doubtful or distrustful of the goodness or sincerity of human motives
   Keith made the *cynical* observation that Jamie's new girlfriend was probably just interested in his money.
   syn: skeptical *ant: idealistic; optimistic*

2. **ambivalent** (am biv´ ə lənt) *adj.* having opposing attitudes or feelings toward a person, thing, or idea; unable to decide
   Doug felt *ambivalent* about his job; although he hated the pressure, he loved the challenge.
   syn: uncertain; wavering *ant: certain; resolute*

3. **demagogue** (dem´ ə gôg) *n.* a leader who appeals to citizens' emotions to obtain power
   The *demagogue* evoked the sympathy of the public to justify his crimes in office.
   syn: rabble-rouser

4. **demure** (di myoor´) *adj.* quiet and modest; reserved
   Her *demure* behavior was really a ruse to cover up her criminal nature.
   syn: prim *ant: indiscreet*

5. **intrepid** (in trep´ ĭd) *adj.* without fear; brave
   The *intrepid* warrior did not even flinch when the tiger leapt from the tree.
   syn: bold; fearless *ant: cowardly*

6. **destitute** (des´ ti tōōt) *adj.* extremely poor; lacking necessities like food and shelter
   Because they had no insurance, they were left *destitute* when their house burned down.
   syn: impoverished; penniless *ant: affluent*

7. **erudite** (er´ yə dīt) *adj.* scholarly; learned
   Not much of a scholar, Justin was intimidated by his *erudite* girlfriend.
   syn: educated *ant: unlettered; illiterate*

8. **dilemma** (di lem´ ə) *n.* a choice between two unpleasant or difficult options
   Whether to repair my old car or purchase a new one was a real *dilemma.*

9. **culmination** (kul mə nā´ shən) *n.* the highest point of attainment; the end or climax
Winning the state tournament was the *culmination* of a great basketball season.
syn: apex *ant: nadir*

10. **concur** (kən kûr´) *v.* to be of the same opinion; to agree with
I *concur* that we should keep this meeting short.
syn: support; agree *ant: dispute; differ*

EXERCISE I—Words in Context

From the list below, supply the words needed to complete the paragraph. Some words will not be used.

concur **intrepid** **cynical** **destitute**
dilemma **ambivalent** **culmination**

A. One year after the __________ of the second Mineral War, the surviving inhabitants of the Europa mining colony endured __________ living conditions. The chief engineer tried her best to restore the food reprocessing system, but, owing to the lack of replacement parts, the unit could produce only thirty percent of the colony's nutritional needs. Captain Keith remained __________ about leading a few __________ miners on a necessary but dangerous expedition to the old generation plant in the Nova Crater to salvage parts for the rapidly declining life support system. Most of the miners were __________ about their fate at the colony, and Captain Keith would have been lying if he said that he didn't __________ with their pessimistic opinions.

From the list below, supply the words needed to complete the paragraph. Some words will not be used.

culmination **demagogue** **concur** **erudite** **dilemma** **demure**

B. Clayton surprised everyone in Selbyville when he entered the race for mayor. For twenty-six years, he had been the mild-mannered, __________ clerk at the Selbyville Courthouse. Well-versed in history and politics, the __________ Clayton never really struck anyone as having the type of personality required to win an election, let alone become the mayor. Word spread quickly when, during a special pre-election meeting, Clayton stood at the podium and delivered an impressive speech. Every word was loaded with passion, especially when Clayton addressed Selbyville's __________ of accepting or rejecting a controversial landfill. After ten minutes of rhetoric, Clayton had the townspeople shouting their support, and the sentiment continued right through to the election, after which Clayton became the new mayor. Three months later, the citizens of Selbyville discovered that Clayton was just a[n] __________ when construction of the new landfill began, and he mysteriously bought a new speedboat that was well beyond the range of a typical small-town mayor's salary.

EXERCISE II—Sentence Completion

Complete the sentence in a way that shows you understand the meaning of the italicized vocabulary word.

1. Your *cynical* attitude makes other people…

2. When forced to be in public, the *demure* Kelly…

3. Now *destitute*, the bankrupt broker lives…

4. The *erudite* professor occasionally lost the attention of the students because…

5. Manny was *ambivalent* about taking the new job because…

6. Stranded behind enemy lines, the *intrepid* soldier…

7. A *demagogue* like Hitler can successfully convince people to…

8. The parents would not *concur* with Dharma's decision to…

9. The *culmination* of the symphony's season occurred at…

10. A *dilemma* at work can force a person to…

EXERCISE III—Roots, Prefixes, and Suffixes

Study the entries and answer the questions that follow.

The root *fid* means "faith" or "trust."
The root *form* means "shape."
The root *crea* means "create, make."
The prefix *re* means "again."
The suffix *tion* means "the act of."
The prefix *re* means "back" or "again."
The prefix *con* means "with."

A. *Using literal translations as guidance, define the following words without using a dictionary:*

1. reformation	4. re-creation
2. reverted	5. fidelity
3. malformed	6. confide

B. *Infidelity* is ______________________________.

C. The Marine Corps' motto, "Semper Fidelis," means ______________________________.

D. List as many words as you can think of that contain the roots *fid* and *form*.

EXERCISE IV—Inference

Complete the sentences by inferring information about the italicized word from its context.

A. When Cynthia sees a *destitute* child who cannot afford new clothing, she usually…

B. If a *demagogue* gets elected, the citizens might…

C. During the battle, the *intrepid* soldier will probably volunteer to…

EXERCISE V—Writing

Here is a writing prompt similar to the one you will find on the writing portion of the SAT.

Plan and write an essay on the following statement:

> They that can give up essential liberty to obtain a little temporary safety deserve neither liberty nor safety.
> – Benjamin Franklin,
> *Historical Review of Pennsylvania*, 1759

Assignment: In a well-organized essay, refute or defend Franklin's point of view. Be certain to support your position by discussing an example (or examples) from current events, science and technology, or your experience and observation.

Thesis: Write a *one-sentence* response to the above assignment. Make certain this single sentence offers a clear statement of your position.
Example: When the nation is at high risk of attack, the government should be allowed to create temporary policies to aid in defense, even if they restrict certain liberties.

-or-

Our government cannot establish any laws that undermine our civil liberties, regardless of the degree of threat to our country.

Organizational Plan: If your thesis is the point on which you want to end, where does your essay need to begin? List the points of development that are inevitable in leading your reader from your beginning point to your end point. This list is your outline.

Draft: Use your thesis as both your beginning and your end. Following your outline, write a good first draft of your essay. Remember to support all your points with examples, facts, references to reading, etc.

Review and Revise: Exchange essays with a classmate. Using the scoring guide for Word Choice on page 209, score your partner's essay (while he or she scores yours). Focus on the word choice and use of language conventions. If necessary, rewrite your essay to improve the word choice and the use of language.

Improving Paragraphs

Read the following passage and then answer the multiple-choice questions that follow. The questions will require you to make decisions regarding the revision of the reading selection. Consider yourself a modern editor faced with this ancient language; your job is to bring the passage up to date.

THE HISTORY OF BEL

(1) The Babylonians had an idol called Bel, and there were spent upon him every day twelve great measures of fine flour, and forty sheep, and six vessels of wine. (2) And the king worshipped it, and went daily to adore it; but Daniel worshipped his own God.

(3) And the king said unto him: "Why dost not thou worship Bel?" (4) Who answered and said: "Because I may not worship idols made with hands, but the living God, who hath created the heaven and the earth, and hath sovereignty over all flesh."

(5) Then said the king unto him: "Thinkest thou not that Bel is a living God? (6) Seest thou not how much he eateth and drinketh every day?" (7) Then Daniel smiled, and said: "O king, be not deceived, for this is but clay within, and brass without, and did never eat or drink any thing."

(8) So the king was wroth, and called for his priests and said unto them: "If ye tell me not who this is that devoureth these expenses, ye shall die. (9) But if ye can certify me that Bel devoureth them, then Daniel shall die, for he hath spoken blasphemously against Bel." (10) And Daniel said unto the king, "Let it be according to thy word." (11) Now the priests of Bel were three score and ten, besides their wives and children; and the king went with Daniel into the temple of Bel.

(12) So Bel's priests said: "Lo, we go out, but thou, O king, set on the meat, and make ready the wine, and shut the door fast, and seal it with thine own signet. (13) And to-morrow, when thou comest in, if thou findest not that Bel hath eaten up all, we will suffer death; or else Daniel that speaketh falsely against us."

(14) And they little regarded it; for under the table they had made a privy entrance, whereby they entered in continually, and consumed those things.

(15) So when they were gone forth, the king set meats before Bel. (16) Now Daniel had Commanded his servants to bring ashes, and those they strewed throughout all the temple, in the presence of the king alone; then went they out, and shut the door, and sealed it with the king's signet, and so departed.

(17) Now in the night came the priests with their wives and children (as they were wont to do), and did eat and drink up all.

(18) In the morning betime the king arose, and Daniel with him. (19) And the king said: "Daniel, are the seals whole?" (20) And he said: "Yea, O king, they be whole." (21) And as soon as he had opened the door, the king looked upon the table, and cried with a loud voice: "Great art thou, O Bel, and with thee is no deceit at all."

(22) Then laughed Daniel, and held the king that he should not go in, and said: "Behold now the pavement, and mark well whose footsteps are these." (23) And the king said: "I see the footsteps of men, women, and children."

(24) And then the king was angry, and took the priests with their wives and children, who showed him the privy doors where they came in, and consumed such things as were upon the table.

(25) Therefore the king slew them, and delivered Bel into Daniel's power, who destroyed him and his temple.

1. Which choice would best improve the language in paragraphs 1 and 2?
   A. Combine them.
   B. Replace *measures* with *bowls.*
   C. Delete all "ands."
   D. Eliminate the second paragraph.
   E. Make verbs current or delete archaic usage.

2. How would you translate *So the king was wroth* (sentence 8) into contemporary English?
   A. The king was reluctant.
   B. The king was angry.
   C. The king was confused.
   D. The king was determined.
   E. The king was relaxed.

3. Which revision would best clarify the phrase *three score and ten* in sentence 11?
   A. Eliminate it.
   B. Replace *three score and ten* with roman numerals.
   C. Use the number seventy.
   D. Capitalize *three score and ten.*
   E. Put a period after *ten.*

4. How can the narrative of the last four paragraphs be improved?
   A. Combine the paragraphs and eliminate the dialogue.
   B. Simplify the language and sentence structure.
   C. Eliminate the reference to ashes.
   D. Specify the food and meats left for Bel.
   E. Eliminate the killing of the priests and their families.

5. Which choice is the best revision of sentence 25?
   A. So he killed them and handed him into Daniel's authority and he destroyed him.
   B. For their deceit, the king slew the priests and their families and gave Daniel the authority to destroy the statue of Bel.
   C. He thus had them slain, with Bel delivered unto the power of Daniel that did destroy him.
   D. Thus did Daniel destroy the idol even as the king slew the priests and their families that did deceive him.
   E. They were killed and the statue was destroyed by the king and Daniel.

REVIEW

Lessons 1 – 7

EXERCISE I – Sentence Completion

Choose the best pair of words to complete the sentence. Most choices will fit grammatically and will even make sense logically, but you must choose the pair that best fits the idea of the sentence.

Note that these words are not taken directly from lessons in this book. This exercise is intended to replicate the sentence completion portion of the SAT.

1. It was quite ____________ that one of the world's most ardent _________ of jogging for health succumbed to a heart attack while running on his personal track.
   A. emphatic, adherents
   B. ironic, advocates
   C. impersonal, supporters
   D. ridiculous, practitioners
   E. comical, writers

2. That newspaper has the facts completely _____________; I think I am going to __________ my subscription.
   A. misaligned, quit
   B. false, renew
   C. incorrect, rescind
   D. wrong, cancel
   E. backwards, annul

3. When you _____________ your income tax for next year, make sure to include any items that would reduce your tax __________.
   A. do, benefits
   B. figure, dependencies
   C. calculate, burden
   D. know, liabilities
   E. take, withdrawals

4. Even many __________ of suntans now realize that tanning booths probably __________ the skin more than the sun itself and, consequently, avoid them.
   A. devotees, misalign
   B. admirers, damage
   C. opponents, destroy
   D. owners, scar
   E. advocates, alter

5. After one year of marriage, Samuel's __________ views about a woman's proper place being in the home were replaced with more __________ views.
   A. incorrect, believable
   B. chauvinistic, worldly
   C. dumb, wise
   D. confusing, startling
   E. antiquated, enlightened

6. The __________ sprinkler system unexpectedly failed during the fire, and the resulting __________ totally ravaged the entire block of apartment buildings.
   A. modern, conflagration
   B. ancient, flames
   C. useless, fire
   D. poor, damage
   E. new, problems

7. Paul thought the computer __________ was __________, but it turned out that the entire machine was ruined beyond repair.
   A. switch, non-functional
   B. hookup, perfect
   C. distortion, mandatory
   D. malfunction, inconsequential
   E. problem, serious

8. The long-standing __________ between the two baseball players became even more __________ when they were forced to play on the same team.
   A. animosity, rancorous
   B. hatred, hateful
   C. respect, obvious
   D. concern, apparent
   E. feelings, pronounced

EXERCISE II – Crossword Puzzle

Use the clues to complete the crossword puzzle. The answers consist of vocabulary words from lessons 1 through 7.

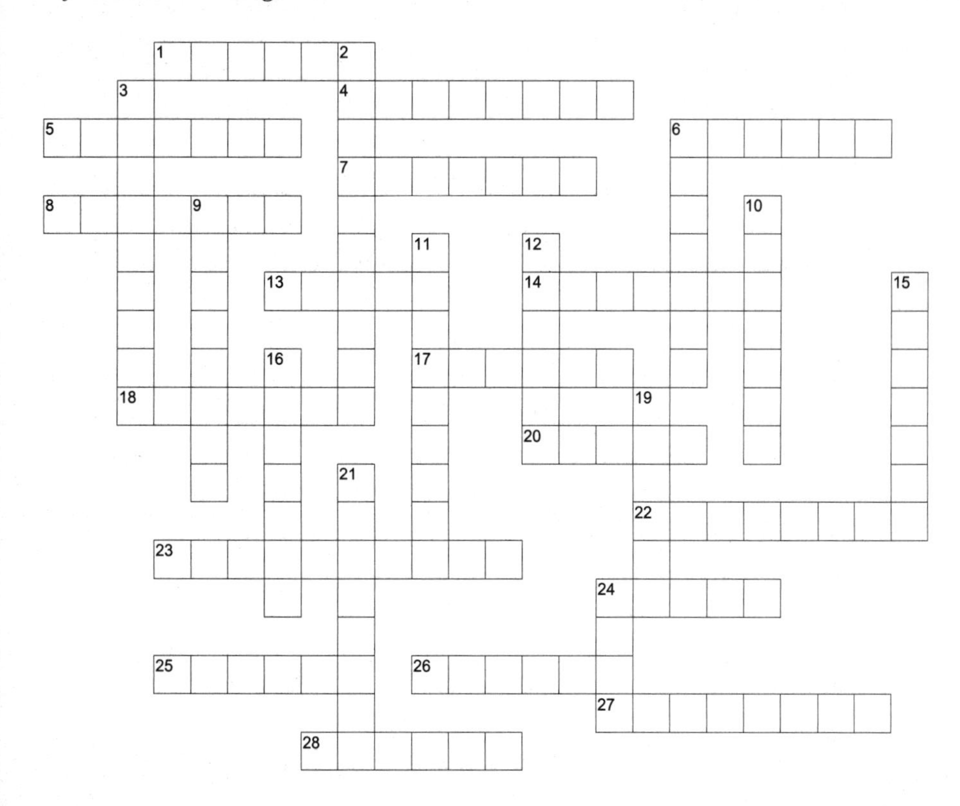

Across

1. outspoken
4. disgrace
5. secretive
6. indifference
7. scholarly
8. fort
13. disorder
14. to calm
17. hatred
18. to erase
20. to praise
22. trust
23. having opposing attitudes
24. lingo
25. easy to teach
26. modest
27. recklessness
28. confident

Down

2. amateur
3. short-tempered
6. unyielding
9. fearless
10. merciful
11. to banish
12. tactless
15. reveal
16. dull
19. agree
21. hated thing
24. to help in crime

Lesson Eight

1. **abate** (ə bāt´) *v.* to lessen in violence or intensity
When the winds *abated*, the helicopter was able to land.
syn: subside; decrease *ant: intensify; increase*

2. **decorum** (di kôr´ əm) *n.* conformity to accepted standards of conduct; proper behavior
The usually restless toddler surprised everyone with his *decorum* during the ceremony.
syn: propriety *ant: inappropriateness*

3. **abhor** (ab hôr´) *v.* to detest; to hate strongly
I *abhor* doing my laundry, so I have it professionally cleaned.
syn: despise; loathe *ant: love; adore*

4. **dole** (dōl) *v.* to distribute; to give out sparingly
At the crowded Red Cross shelter, food was *doled* out carefully to the earthquake victims.
ant: hoard

5. **gamut** (gam´ ət) *n.* the whole range or extent
Carmela's *gamut* of friends includes both overzealous socialists and greedy capitalists.

6. **extrovert** (ek´ strə vûrt) *n.* one who is outgoing; one who is energized rather than drained by interactions with others
As an *extrovert*, Liz loved parties and preferred entertaining to spending a quiet night alone.
ant: introvert

7. **droll** (drōl) *adj.* amusing in an odd or whimsical way
Xander had a *droll* manner of telling stories that kept everyone entertained.
syn: quaint

8. **duplicity** (dōō plis´ i tē) *n.* intentional deceit in speech or conduct
His *duplicity* became obvious when he absent-mindedly arranged to meet both his wife and his mistress at the same restaurant.
syn: deception *ant: straightforwardness*

9. **effigy** (ef´ i jē) *n.* a crude dummy or image representing a hated person or group
The repressed people burned an *effigy* of their tyrannous dictator.

10. **austere** (ô stîr′) *adj.* stern; severe; plain
    The judge was as *austere* in her courtroom manner as she was in her lifestyle and dress.
    syn: strict; unadorned *ant: luxurious; indulgent*

EXERCISE I—Words in Context

From the list below, supply the words needed to complete the paragraph. Some words will not be used.

droll gamut effigy austere duplicity abhor extrovert

A. Monique was a[n] __________ who loved dealing with people, but she never thought that she would satisfy her need for socializing by selling used cars. She always __________ salespeople, but after becoming one, Monique realized that only a fraction of the __________ of salespeople indulge in the __________ and false promises that make dissatisfied customers angry enough to burn __________ of them.

From the list below, supply the words needed to complete the paragraph. Some words will not be used.

abate decorum dole abhor droll austere duplicity

B. Typhoon Paka hammered the island of Guam for twelve hours before the winds __________. Gusts over two hundred miles an hour devastated the previously green island, creating __________ living conditions for residents in the weeks to come, especially for the estimated five thousand people who lost their homes. Residents able to witness Paka in action were astounded by the serious but almost __________ sight of Paka's invisible forces tossing around automobiles, dumpsters, and palm trees as though they were children's toys. In the days following Paka, residents adhered to traditional post-typhoon __________ by cleaning up hundreds of tons of debris, checking on the condition of friends and neighbors, repairing property, and, because of the lack of electricity, hosting mass barbecues before food perished in warm refrigerators. Luckily, food was not in short supply, but water had to be __________ out by several agencies in the weeks following the tempest.

EXERCISE II—Sentence Completion

Complete the sentence in a way that shows you understand the meaning of the italicized vocabulary word.

1. Three days after the shipwreck, the captain *doled* out...
2. The peasants burned the *effigy* of the Duke because...
3. The comedian's *droll* attempt to impersonate the president caused...
4. The *austere* conditions of the Alaskan tundra caused the settlers to...
5. Othello trusted his wife until Iago's *duplicity* made the Moor think that...
6. Until the typhoon *abated*, the supply ships could not...
7. Kenyon, an *extrovert*, called all her friends and...
8. Having no time for *decorum*, the federal agents charged into the ballroom and...
9. If I did not *abhor* pickles, I would be sad that...
10. The *gamut* of people on the elevator included...

EXERCISE III—Roots, Prefixes, and Suffixes

Study the entries and answer the questions that follow.

The roots *frag* and *fract* mean "break."
The root *chrono* means "time."
The suffix *ment* means "the result of" or "product of the action."
The suffix *logical* means "ordered by."
The prefix *re* means "back, again."

A. *Using literal translations as guidance, define the following words without using a dictionary:*

1. chronic
2. fragment
3. fragile
4. chronological
5. chronicle
6. refract

B. A character answering a telephone during the play *Julius Caesar* would be an *anachronism* because ________________________________.

C. A *fragmentary* report is one that is ____________________________.

D. List as many words as you can think of that contain the forms *frag*, *fract*, and *chrono*.

EXERCISE IV—Inference

Complete the sentences by inferring information about the italicized word from its context.

A. To fashion a detailed *effigy* of the mayor, the angry townspeople might…

B. As the wagon train moved west, conditions on the plains became so *austere* that the pioneers…

C. If you *abhor* getting muddy and dirty, then you should probably not…

EXERCISE V—Critical Reading

Below is a pair of reading passages followed by several multiple-choice questions similar to the ones you will encounter on the SAT. Carefully read both passages and choose the best answer to each of the questions.

Both of these passages are arguments in favor of the American Revolution against Great Britain. The first comes from the initial pamphlet in Thomas Paine's series entitled The American Crisis, *which uses emotional appeals to persuade the reader. The second comes from the* Declaration of Independence, *which takes on a more rational, logical aspect.*

Passage 1

These are the times that try men's souls. The summer soldier and the sunshine patriot will in this crisis, shrink from the service of his country; but he that stands it NOW, deserves the love and thanks of man and woman. Tyranny, like hell, is not easily conquered; yet we have this conso-
5 lation with us, that the harder the conflict, the more glorious the triumph. What we obtain too cheap, we esteem too lightly; 'tis dearness only that gives everything its proper value. Heaven knows how to put a proper price upon its goods; and it would be strange indeed, if so celestial an article as FREEDOM should not be highly rated. Britain, with an army to enforce her
10 tyranny, has declared that she has a right (not only to TAX), but "to BIND us in ALL CASES WHATSOEVER," and if being bound in that manner, is not slavery, then is there not such a thing as slavery upon earth. Even the expression is impious, for so unlimited a power can belong only to God…

I have as little superstition in me as any man living, but my secret
15 opinion has ever been, and still is, that God Almighty will not give up a people to military destruction, or leave them unsupportedly to perish, who have so earnestly and so repeatedly sought to avoid the calamities of war, by every decent method which wisdom could invent. Neither have I so much of the infidel in me, as to suppose that he has relinquished the
20 government of the world, and given us up to the care of devils; and as I do not, I cannot see on what grounds the king of Britain can look up to heaven for help against us: a common murderer, a highwayman, or housebreaker, has as good a pretense as he…

Passage 2

When in the Course of human events, it becomes necessary for one people to dissolve the political bands which have connected them with another, and to assume among the powers of the earth, the separate and equal station to which the Laws of Nature and of Nature's God entitle
5 them, a decent respect to the opinions of mankind requires that they should declare the causes which impel them to the separation....The history of the present King of Great Britain is a history of repeated injuries and usurpations, all having in direct object the establishment of absolute Tyranny over these States. To prove this, let facts be submitted to a candid
10 world.

He has refused his Assent to Laws the most wholesome and necessary for the public good.

He has forbidden his Governors to pass Laws of immediate and pressing importance....

15 He has called together legislative bodies at places unusual, uncomfortable, and distant from the depository of their public Records, for the sole purpose of fatiguing them into compliance with his measures.

He has dissolved Representative Houses repeatedly, for opposing with manly firmness his invasions on the rights of the people....

20 He has erected a multitude of New Offices, and sent hither swarms of Officers to harass our people and eat out their substance.

He has kept among us in times of peace Standing Armies without the Consent of our legislatures....

He has plundered our seas, ravaged our Coasts, burnt our towns, and
25 destroyed the lives of our people....

In every stage of these Oppressions We have Petitioned for Redress in the most humble terms. Our repeated petitions have been answered only by repeated injury.

1. In the context of the first passage, what is the most appropriate definition of *dearness* as it appears in line 6?
   A. fondness
   B. expense
   C. endearment
   D. glory
   E. courage

2. In the first passage, the purpose of the simile in line 4 is most likely
   A. to honor the religious occasion of this essay.
   B. to show the ease with which the Americans would defeat Britain.
   C. to give the American-British dispute a more sharply moral tone.
   D. to introduce the difficulty of overcoming temptation.
   E. to add the rhetorical weight of an expletive to the sentence.

3. The overall tone of the first passage can best be described as
   A. rational.
   B. hysterical.
   C. morose.
   D. emotional.
   E. pragmatic.

4. According to the last paragraph of the first passage, the author expects a great deal of assistance for the American cause to originate in
   A. the "decent method" of wisdom.
   B. superstitious practices.
   C. divine intervention.
   D. the crimes of the British king.
   E. the good will from the American desire to avoid war.

5. What is the effect of the parallel structure used at the beginning of paragraphs 2-8, in the second passage?
   A. It focuses the blame squarely on the British king.
   B. It inflames the passions of the reader.
   C. It outlines the various misdeeds of the British government.
   D. It emphasizes the suffering of the American colonies.
   E. It lends a grave, rational tone to the entire passage.

6. Based on the context of the second passage, the best definition of *usurpations* (line 8) is
   A. injustices.
   B. seizures.
   C. lies.
   D. treacheries.
   E. slanders.

7. Who is the primary audience of the second passage?
   A. the American colonists
   B. the king of England
   C. the American press
   D. the French ambassador
   E. the world at large

8. Which word below is used in the second passage to make the British troops seem less human?
    A. "Standing" (line 22)
    B. "substance" (line 21)
    C. "swarms" (line 20)
    D. "burnt" (line 24)
    E. "repeated" (line 28)

9. What is the primary difference between the tones of the two passages?
    A. Passage One appeals more to the logic of the reader than Passage Two.
    B. Passage Two contains fewer attempts to engage the reader emotionally than Passage One.
    C. Passage One reacts angrily to the misdeeds of the British king, while Passage Two merely registers objections.
    D. Passage Two avoids reference to divine intervention, while Passage One invokes God's aid in behalf of the American cause.
    E. Passage One uses shorter sentences to increase the emotional pace, and Passage Two seems to be written to a more literate audience.

10. Which of the following statements most accurately describes the relationship between the two passages?
    A. Passage One expresses the emotional urgency of the colonial situation, while Passage Two expresses the rational conclusions generated by that situation.
    B. Passage Two presents the complaints of the colonies in much less detail than Passage One does.
    C. Passage One is more detached than Passage Two.
    D. Details in the two passages reveal that the authors had dissenting opinions about the colonial situation.
    E. Both passages expect the reader to arrive at his or her own conclusion.

Lesson Nine

1. **emulate** (em´ yə lāt) *v.* to strive to be equal to; to imitate
   Jonas *emulated* his older brother by pursuing a career in the same business.
   syn: copy

2. **sere** (sēr) *adj.* dry and withered
   After two weeks without water, the *sere* plant broke at the stem.
   syn: desiccated; arid *ant: lush*

3. **enhance** (en hans´) *v.* to increase the value or beauty of something
   The soft, shimmering moonlight *enhanced* the beauty of the sparkling lake.
   syn: improve; heighten *ant: diminish; decrease*

4. **contrite** (kən trīt´) *adj.* feeling regret for having committed some wrongdoing
   The *contrite* child wished she had never thought of playing baseball near the greenhouse.
   syn: repentant; remorseful *ant: shameless; unrepentant*

5. **magnanimous** (mag nan´ ə məs) *adj.* noble; generous in forgiving; free from petty feelings or acts
   Allowing the man who had insulted him to stay for dinner was a *magnanimous* gesture on Robert's part.
   syn: generous *ant: petty; mean*

6. **enunciate** (i nun´ sē āt) *v.* to state clearly and distinctly; to pronounce
   The speech teacher constantly reminded her students to *enunciate* their words carefully.
   syn: articulate

7. **collaborate** (kə lab´ ə rāt) *v.* to work with another toward a goal
   The lyricist and composer *collaborated* on the stage musical.
   syn: cooperate

8. **impound** (im pownd´) *v.* to confine; to retain in legal custody
   The police *impounded* Dave's car after they found traces of cocaine on the upholstery.
   syn: confiscate *ant: release*

9. **impeccable** (im pek´ ə bəl) *adj.* faultless; without sin or blemish
   Keith's appearance was *impeccable*, from his handsome shoes to his neatly combed hair.
   syn: immaculate; faultless; irreproachable *ant: fallible; blameworthy*

10. **evoke** (i vōk´) *v.* to summon forth
The comedian was unable to *evoke* much of a response from the crowd.
syn: conjure up; elicit

11. **inane** (in ān´) *adj.* without sense or meaning; silly
Still dazed from the head injury, Catherine made only *inane* comments.
syn: foolish; insipid *ant: significant; meaningful*

12. **unctuous** (ungk´ chōō əs) *adj.* exaggeratedly or insincerely polite
The salesman kept calling me "ma'am" in such an *unctuous* tone that I did not trust him for a minute.
syn: oily *ant: genuine; sincere*

13. **expatriate** (eks pā´ trē ət) *n.* someone who chooses to live outside of, or renounce, his or her native country
Although T. S. Eliot was born in America, he was an *expatriate* for most of his life and is often considered British.

14. **frowzy** (frow´ zē) *adj.* unkempt
The lady's *frowzy* hair was so tangled that it looked like Spanish moss.
syn: slovenly *ant: tidy*

15. **heinous** (hā´ nəs) *adj.* hatefully or shockingly evil
The jury was shocked by the young woman's *heinous* crimes.
syn: abhorrent; horrid

EXERCISE I—Words in Context

From the list below, supply the words needed to complete the paragraph. Some words will not be used.

magnanimous	**impeccable**	**impound**	**contrite**
expatriate	**emulate**	**collaborate**	

A. "Don't __________ me, kid—unless you want to spend time in the slammer, too," Buddy laughed as he put his hands in the air and glanced around. "But if you're really interested, maybe we can __________ on familiarizing you with the racing community."

Lucas didn't return his uncle's smirk. He instead directed his __________ expression to the table and fiddled with the phone cord. Lucas never really adapted to conversing through a sheet of Plexiglas, and the tinny sound of Buddy's musing through the two-way intercom made him uncomfortable. Lucas came to the prison only because the police were going to __________ Buddy's car if no one removed it from the credit union parking lot, and Lucas thought that he was being __________ by mentioning that he, like Buddy, had an interest in horse racing.

From the list below, supply the words needed to complete the paragraph. Some words will not be used.

evoke	**expatriate**	**heinous**	**frowzy**
inane	**sere**	**enhance**	**enunciate**

B. Jerry squinted and ran his hand through his __________ mop of hair. The Pacific sun was already high in the sky, and he had a lot of work to accomplish before his guests arrived that evening. Originally from a Minnesota dairy, Jerry had lived on the tiny Micronesian island for over sixteen years. He never really considered himself to be a[n] __________, but then again, he didn't ever plan to return to United States, either. Thinking that it might be a good idea to __________ his front yard before his visitors arrived, Jerry grabbed a machete and walked to the coconut grove in front of his shack. Huffing, Jerry chopped at the __________, withered fronds hanging against the trunks of the palm trees. When he finished cutting the fronds, he gathered the stray coconuts—some months old—and piled them in the corner of his yard. The yard looked sharp, even with Jerry's dilapidated shack in the background. As a bonus, Jerry decided to place two rows of tiki-torches along the path to the shack. Jerry thought that such trinkets were __________, but he wanted his two nieces from Cleveland to get the total island experience.

From the list below, supply the words needed to complete the paragraph. Some words will not be used.

enunciate **evoke** **expatriate** **unctuous** **heinous** **impeccable**

C. Jordan sat at the helm and surveyed the broken radio before speaking to Candace.

"This is not going to be easy. You're going to have to __________ all the strength you have in order to succeed."

In her typical sarcastic manner, Candace responded to Jordan in a[n] __________ tone. "Oh, really? Thank goodness you told me; I thought that swimming two miles through an oil slick would be easy!"

"That's enough," snapped Candace as she walked over to the porthole and looked at the horizon. The line where the earth met the sky was tilted by at least seven or eight degrees; the *Nittany* was definitely taking on water. The wounded tanker in the distance wasn't doing much better; from the *Nittany's* bridge, Jordan could tell where the tanker's hull had ruptured by a black swirl slowly meandering through the crystal clear water.

"Do you remember what you're doing?"

Still annoyed, Candace __________ the directions as though she were reciting letters in an elementary school spelling bee: "Swim to the reef, walk to the shore, find the radio house, neutralize the guard, and call Boswell. Right?"

"Right," said Jordan. "Be sure to give him the proper coordinates; I'm not going down with the ship."

"Oh, don't worry," snapped Candace. "Any shark that eats you will immediately spit you back out."

"Ha-ha. Thanks for the __________ image of my certain death."

"Oh, relax. Once we get out of this I'll treat you to a[n] __________ lobster dinner on Maui. See ya later!" With that, Candace walked out of the bridge and jumped over the handrail. Jordan didn't even hear the splash.

EXERCISE II—Sentence Completion

Complete the sentence in a way that shows you understand the meaning of the italicized vocabulary word.

1. The *sere* peach tree finally collapsed after several months without…

2. Some people try to *enhance* their looks by…

3. Police *impounded* Shauna's car because she…

4. The bandit's *heinous* record included the crimes of…

5. Known to be a shrine of *impeccable* art, Marlene's home was filled with…

6. The *expatriate* writer decided never to return to…

7. In his typical *magnanimous* manner, Richard ignored his sister's habitual…

8. Your *inane* behavior is not acceptable during…

9. The *frowzy* old man had obviously been living…

10. Please *enunciate* your words clearly so that everyone will…

11. Expect the *unctuous* greeting of the maitre d' if you…

12. The old medium attempted to *evoke* the spirit of…

13. The Army and the Air Force must *collaborate* during…

14. The *contrite* young thief apologized for…

15. Maggie *emulates* her older sister by…

EXERCISE III—Roots, Prefixes, and Suffixes

Study the entries and answer the questions that follow.

The root *cogn* means "know" or "think."
The root *carn* means "flesh."
The root *vor* means "eat."
The prefix *in* means "not." (It can also mean "in.")
The prefix *re* means "again."

A. *Using literal translations as guidance, define the following words without using a dictionary:*

1. incognito	4. carnivore
2. cogitation	5. carnivorous
3. cognizant	6. reincarnate

B. In the Latin phrase "cogito ergo sum," *ergo* means "therefore" and *sum* means "I am." What do you suppose the entire phrase means?

C. A carnival used to refer specifically to a holiday or holidays that took place just before the start of Lent. Since Lent was a time when eating meat was forbidden, what do you suppose *carnival* meant?

D. List as many words as you can think of that contain the forms *cogn, carn.*

EXERCISE IV—Inference

Complete the sentences by inferring information about the italicized word from its context.

A. Kayla wants to *enhance* the appearance of her room, so she should…

B. Despite her lifelong stutter, Tara *enunciated* her speeches so well that she became…

C. Dalton's older brother is a fireman, and Dalton used to *emulate* him by…

EXERCISE V—Writing

Here is a writing prompt similar to the one you will find on the writing portion of the SAT.

Plan and write an editorial for your school newspaper on the issue described below:

> If there were in the world today any large number of people who desired their own happiness more than they desired the unhappiness of others, we could have paradise in a few years.
>
> – Bertrand Russell

Assignment: After facing several student disciplinary problems related to the dress code, the administration of your school has decided to mandate school uniforms for students but not for the faculty. Using the quotation as your inspiration, express your opinion on the issue.

Thesis: Write a *one-sentence* response to the above assignment. Make certain this single sentence offers a clear statement of your position. The sentence should appear early in your first paragraph.
Example: The administration is subjecting the entire student body to unfair, discriminatory standards because it does not want to deal with a few problem students.

Organizational Plan: If your thesis is the point on which you want to end, where does your essay need to begin? List the points of development that are inevitable in leading your reader from your beginning point to your end point. This list is your outline.

Draft: Use your thesis as both your beginning and your end. Following your outline, write a good first draft of your essay. Remember to support all your points with examples, facts, references to reading, etc.

Review and Revise: Exchange essays with a classmate. Using the Holistic scoring guide on page 210, score your partner's essay (while he or she scores yours). If necessary, rewrite your essay to correct the problems noted by your partner.

Identifying Sentence Errors

Identify the errors in the following sentences. If the sentence contains no error, select answer E.

1. High levels (A) of air pollution (B) causes (C) damage to (D) the respiratory tract. No error (E)

2. Sally and Jane (A) goes (B) to the mall (C) every day (D). No error (E)

3. Each flower, (A) tree, (B) shrub, and bush (C) need watering (D). No error (E)

4. A young couple (A) was (B) strolling (C) through the park (D) while holding hands. No error (E)

5. The number (A) of (B) volunteers for the military (C) is declining (D). No error (E)

Improving Sentences

The underlined portion of each sentence below contains some flaw. Select the answer choice that best corrects the flaw.

6. John was not only a talented student but also was a great athlete.
   A. not only a talented student, but also a great athlete.
   B. only a talented student, but also was a great athlete.
   C. not only a talented student, but also was great.
   D. not only a talented student, but was also a great athlete.
   E. a talented student, a great athlete.

7. My niece could not be persuaded that giving is as much a joy as receiving.
   A. persuaded that giving is as much a joy as to receive.
   B. persuaded that to give is as much a joy as receiving.
   C. convinced that giving is as much a joy as to receive.
   D. made to feel that giving is as much a joy as to receive.
   E. No revision needed.

8. Our leaders believe and live by the law.
   A. rust and live by the law.
   B. believe in and live by the law.
   C. believe in and live the law.
   D. obey in and live by the law.
   E. trust and obey by the law.

9. The Earth is bluer than any planet in our solar system.
   A. The Earth is bluer than any planet's in our solar system.
   B. The Earth is bluer than a planet in our system.
   C. The Earth is bluer than any other planet in our solar system.
   D. The Earth is bluer than any planet in the solar system.
   E. No revision needed.

10. All pottery is not antique.
   A. Not all pottery is antique.
   B. All pottery is antique.
   C. All clay pottery is not antique.
   D. All clay pottery is antique.
   E. All clay pottery is not new.

Lesson Ten

1. **expound** (ik spownd´) *v.* to explain in detail; to clarify
Closing the Bible, the minister *expounded* the passage he had just read.
syn: elaborate *ant: muddle; confuse*

2. **cajole** (kə jōl´) *v.* to persuade with false promises and flattery
Despite her best efforts, the mayor could not *cajole* Madame Harris into donating the land to the city.
syn: coax; wheedle *ant: dissuade; deter*

3. **inscrutable** (in skrōō´ tə bəl) *adj.* not easily understood; hard to fathom
The crazed stalker left an *inscrutable* message on my answering machine.
syn: enigmatic *ant: obvious; evident*

4. **balk** (bôk) *v.* to refuse stubbornly or abruptly; to stop short and refuse to go on
Although Paul desperately needed the money, he *balked* at the idea of working for less than minimum wage.
syn: hesitate; object *ant: agree; continue*

5. **acrimony** (a´ krə mō nē) *n.* ill-natured, bitter hostility
Because of his *acrimony*, the old man found himself lonely and friendless.
syn: animosity *ant: friendliness*

6. **dour** (dowr) *adj.* stern and ill-humored
The librarian's *dour* expression and stereotypical bifocals contradicted her tattoos and noisy motorcycle.
syn: forbidding *ant: pleasant*

7. **exult** (ig zult´) *v.* to rejoice; to feel triumphant
When the results were announced, the town wildly *exulted* in its team's victory.
syn: celebrate

8. **omniscient** (om nish´ ənt) *adj.* having unlimited knowledge; all-knowing
Dad described Santa Claus as an *omniscient* old man who knew whether we had been bad or good this year.

9. **feasible** (fē´ zə bəl) *adj.* reasonable; capable of being carried out
Though he is still young, Jeff has a *feasible* plan to participate in the Olympic games.
syn: possible; doable *ant: unworkable*

10. **fiasco** (fē as´ kō) *n.* a complete, ridiculous failure
Our first date was a *fiasco*: I lost a contact lens, we got mugged, and a child threw up on Amber's shoes in the subway.
syn: disaster *ant: success*

11. **métier** (me tyā´) *n.* the work one is especially suited for; one's specialty; an occupation
Justin is a decent singer, but dancing is his real *métier*.
syn: forte *ant: weakness*

12. **fluctuate** (fluk´ chōō āt) *v.* to rise and fall; to vary irregularly
The stock market *fluctuates* so much that it seems silly to get upset when your stock goes down; it will probably go back up tomorrow.
syn: waver; vacillate *ant: stabilize*

13. **harry** (har´ ē) *v.* to annoy or harass
The baby's constant crying began to *harry* the other passengers on the train.
syn: bother; pester *ant: soothe*

14. **incognito** (in kog nē´ tō) *adj.* disguised; pretending not to be oneself
To avoid clamoring fans, the actor donned a disguise and traveled *incognito*.

15. **lethargy** (leth´ ər jē) *n.* lack of energy; sluggishness
The heat and humidity made me sink into the couch, too overwhelmed with *lethargy* to move.
syn: torpor; lassitude *ant: vigor; vitality*

EXERCISE I—Words in Context

From the list below, supply the words needed to complete the paragraph. Some words will not be used.

fluctuate	**cajole**	**expound**	**acrimony**
exult	**inscrutable**	**métier**	**harry**

A. Councilwoman Moore stepped up to the podium. "I don't think I need to __________ my reasons for voting against the proposed construction; I thought that the message was clear enough at the last meeting—when you all opposed it as well. Obviously, someone has __________ a few of you since last month, and your sudden, __________ decision to yield to Beta-Rad Enterprises bothers me a great deal. What happened to the surplus of __________ toward Beta-Rad from the last meeting? Don't you remember how we __________ in our victory over the radioactive waste dump? For two years, we've listened to Beta-Rad execs __________ us, and we finally had the chance to stop it for good. How could the opinions of fifteen people possibly __________ this much?"

From the list below, supply the words needed to complete the paragraph. Some words will not be used.

incognito	**feasible**	**dour**	**fiasco**	**métier**
lethargy	**balk**	**omniscient**	**harry**	

B. "Hey, Jye; I think you've found your __________."

"Could be." Jye glanced up only long enough to catch a glimpse of Neve. Typing rapidly, Jye intermittently glanced at the stack of printed matrixes next to the keyboard. Usually a[n] __________ person who remained hidden in his software-engineer cubicle all day, Jye adopted a manner bordering on cynicism and __________—getting him to do tech support beyond his cubicle walls was often a[n] __________ that created more trouble than it solved. Neve was caught completely off-guard when Jye didn't __________ at the company's request that he test the system's network security by hacking into the company database. Though Jye had his ways, everyone knew that he was the __________ office authority when it came to network security protocol. It simply wouldn't have been __________ to use anyone else to test the integrity of Pentacode's newest software. Additionally, Jye's newfound energy changed his manner so much that he might as well have been __________ to those who didn't see him every day; when his attitude changed, his wardrobe and hairstyle changed as well.

EXERCISE II—Sentence Completion

Complete the sentence in a way that shows you understand the meaning of the italicized vocabulary word.

1. Finally able to dismount from his bicycle, Lance did not *exult* despite…

2. The monkeys native to India sometimes *harry* villagers by…

3. Ann's *lethargy* was not due to the heat; she was simply…

4. Caitlyn, a remarkable writer, found her *métier* as…

5. The wedding went well, but the *acrimony* between the families resulted in…

6. Please *expound* your explanation of…

7. The *inscrutable* actions of the building inspector caused…

8. To avoid a *fiasco* during your camping trip, be sure to…

9. I would have donated money, but I *balked* when I learned that…

10. If the warden were indeed *omniscient*, then he would know that…

11. Uncle Tony was not originally a *dour* man; ten years ago, he…

12. Milton's *fluctuating* condition prevents the doctor from…

13. Not even six years of *cajoling* could convince Mrs. Garcia to…

14. Wary of being discovered by the rebels, the *incognito* Colonel Lito wore…

15. A *feasible* reason for missing work would be…

EXERCISE III—Roots, Prefixes, and Suffixes

Study the entries and answer the questions that follow.

The root *agri* means "field, farming."
The suffixes *ous* and *ose* mean "full of."
The root *bell* means "war."
The root *gere* means "bearing" or "waging."
The prefix *ante* means "before."
The suffix *onomy* means "study of."

A. *Using literal translations as guidance, define the following words without using a dictionary:*

1. antebellum
2. bellicose
3. agriculture
4. belligerent
5. anteroom
6. agronomy

B. The roots *ces* and *ced* mean "to go"; therefore, an *antecedent* is a word that ____________________.

C. An industrial society is characterized by cities and manufacturing; an *agrarian* society is characterized by ______________________________ ____________.

D. List as many words as you can think of that contain the forms *agr* or *ante.*

EXERCISE IV—Inference

Complete the sentences by inferring information about the italicized word from its context.

A. If you *harry* the stray dog, it's quite possible that it will…

B. If an *avid* skier crashes on the slope, you can assume that…

C. Mom must have been *omniscient* if she knew that Derek secretly…

EXERCISE V—Critical Reading

Below is a reading passage followed by several multiple-choice questions similar to the ones you will encounter on the SAT. Carefully read the passage and choose the best answer to each of the questions.

The author of this passage is discussing the unique characteristics of the Victorian Era in Great Britain.

1 Despite its cruel working conditions and mass poverty, Victorian England will always be remembered as a forerunner to the modern industrial society. As an incubator for early industry, 19th century England was the first dominion in the world to experience the cultural byproducts that accompanied advancements in transportation and technology. The resulting cultural shifts spawned a bouquet of unique historical attributes that today classify Victorian England.

2 Railways—the new method of mass land transportation to meet the blooming demands of early mass production—were at the heart of Victorian England's changes. Stimulating industry, railroads inspired advancements in coal mining, iron production, and construction engineering that resulted in better buildings, bridges, and machines; these advancements, in turn, made England the foremost machine-manufacturer in the world.

3 As the demand for industry increased, so did the demand for a working class: skilled artisans, craftsmen, and domestic out-workers who didn't require the construction of more facilities. The boom in skilled workers created a demand for more middle class members, such as doctors, bankers, and lawyers. Manufacturing also caused growth in the middle class due to requirements for educated professionals such as architects, engineers, and owners of industry.

4 The growth and importance of the new working class caused many of the British to question the justification of the existing class structure, in which the upper class appeared to reap the most benefits without having to endure the subhuman conditions of early factories. Realizing that they were crucial to industry, workers demonstrated their importance by organizing strikes in an effort to obtain better wages and working conditions. Forerunners of this movement were the Chartists, who not only wanted to enhance working conditions but also to redesign the government of England. The Chartists failed to change Parliament, but they did succeed in persuading Parliament to pass several acts from 1833 to 1847 that improved working conditions for women and children.

5 The literature of England reflected the new social consciousness of the Victorian period. Mass manufacturing led to cheap publishing, making books available for the increasingly literate masses, regardless of economic class. Owing to the availability of books, novels became popular and the prevalent subjects of literature changed. In a departure from Romantic literature, fiction entertained contemporary affairs and common people instead of ancient legends and kingly heroes. Writers such as Lewis Carroll and Charles Dickens were free to satirize the establishment or to depict the austere lives that many of the working class endured every day.

6 New schools of thought also emerged because of the new, convenient way to distribute information, often to the benefit of the working class. Activists such as the Chartists explored new or better forms of government, drawing ideas from people and events throughout the world, one of whom was Karl Marx. In 1840, Karl Marx wrote the *Communist Manifesto* while workers were at the depths of misery. Marx's ideas favored the strength of the workers rather than the ingenuity of industry leaders, which immediately became an inspiration to many deprived workers. The American Revolution also fueled sentiment in Victorian England, especially now that the middle class could read about the exploits of American Revolutionary leaders and their ideas about human equality and inherent rights. Penny magazines, cheap to produce and easy to distribute, helped inflame the passions of the working class. New philosophies emerged as well, some of which exemplified the legitimacy of science. Charles Darwin's *The Origin of Species*, published in 1859, caused sudden doubt in traditional modes of thought; some people embraced Positivism, which states that concrete evidence and scientific laws govern the universe.

7 The changing perspectives of Victorian England also inspired artists and architects to depart from traditional styles. Designers abandoned classical décor for Gothic spires or gaudy embellishments and stained glass windows, creating unique designs that, to this day, many people easily identify as Victorian. Like the dividing social classes, artists also held to different opinions about the role of art. Some artists, threatened by the growth of industry, thought that art should remind people that they are human beings and not machines. Other Victorian artists debated over whether to maintain classical style or to embrace realism. Like literature, new forms of art were in high demand owing to the growing middle-class audience.

8 The railways of Victorian England carried much more than simple cargo and passengers; they carried the sweeping changes that would blanket the world in a new era—the Industrial Age—and it would last more than 200 years, until factories and railways would slowly disintegrate as technology carried humans into the Age of Information. The remnants from the era will continue to stand, however, in the form of Gothic cathedrals, Queen Anne homes, and miles of steel bridges constructed in a time when human effort was meant to be timeless.

1. The primary purpose of this passage is to
   A. explain Victorianism.
   B. discuss the impact of industry on culture.
   C. offer a theory on the "Age of the Railway."
   D. discuss the characteristics of Victorianism.
   E. explain the impact of the railroad.

2. The overall tone of this passage is
   A. informative.
   B. descriptive.
   C. entertaining.
   D. thoughtful.
   E. speculative.

3. As used in paragraph 3, the phrase *domestic out-workers* most likely means
   A. workers who are tame.
   B. outdoor workers.
   C. people who work from their homes.
   D. people who are no longer domestic.
   E. people who do housework for other people.

4. As used in paragraph 5, the term *Romantic* most likely refers to
   A. the condition of being in love.
   B. the time period immediately preceding the Victorian Era.
   C. the art and philosophy of ancient Rome.
   D. a Roman person.
   E. involvement with poetry.

5. According to paragraph 5, which of the following helped the novel to become popular?
   A. inexpensive publishing
   B. the Communists
   C. a more literate population
   D. coal mining
   E. ink production techniques

6. According to this passage, which is *not* one of the advancements due to railroads?
   A. iron production
   B. coal mining
   C. automobile manufacturing
   D. construction engineering
   E. better bridges

7. As used in paragraph 6, Positivism most likely means
   A. always looking on the bright side.
   B. being attracted to the optimistic.
   C. believing experience is the only basis for knowledge.
   D. believing that everything is good.
   E. believing only the good survives.

8. Which of the following is *not* discussed in the passage as contributing to the characteristics of the Victorian age?
   A. new ideas
   B. an increase in industry and machines
   C. art
   D. architecture
   E. lace clothing styles

9. What would make the best title for this passage?
   A. The Characteristics of Victorian England
   B. A Change in Ideas
   C. How Art and Literature Affect People
   D. Communism in England
   E. Political Change By Industry

10. This passage would most likely be found in
    A. a teen magazine.
    B. an encyclopedia of politics.
    C. a British history book.
    D. an American history book.
    E. a book on architecture.

Lesson Eleven

1. **epistle** (i pis´ əl) *n.* a letter or literary composition in letter form
Brian spent years writing lengthy, unsent *epistles* to his old girlfriend.

2 **avid** (av´ id) *adj.* enthusiastic; extremely interested
Dori was such an *avid* reader that I had a hard time recommending a title she had not yet read.
syn: voracious; eager *ant: apathetic*

3. **gadfly** (gad´ flī) *n.* an irritating and persistent person
I tried to lose Judy, an obnoxious *gadfly*, in the crowd, but she stuck to me with unbearable closeness.
syn: nuisance; pest

4. **humility** (hyōō mil´ i tē) *n.* absence of vanity; humbleness
Even though Jo is a celebrated author, she's the picture of *humility* and never brags.
syn: modesty *ant: vanity; arrogance*

5. **dolorous** (dō´ lə rəs) *adj.* exhibiting sorrow or pain
The song was so *dolorous* that Dolores found it difficult not to cry.
syn: mournful *ant: joyous*

6. **gargantuan** (gär gan´ chōō ən) *adj.* of huge or extraordinary size and power
Milltown's players were *gargantuan* compared with the small guys on our team.
syn: gigantic; huge *ant: tiny*

7. **arduous** (är´ jōō əs) *adj.* difficult; requiring much effort
Refinishing the old bookcase proved an *arduous* task, but the results were well worth it.
syn: strenuous; laborious *ant: easy; unchallenging*

8. **affable** (af´ ə bel) *adj.* friendly; agreeable; easy to talk to
The *affable* old man never lacked for visitors.
syn: amiable; good-natured *ant: disagreeable; irascible*

9. **grandiloquent** (gran dil´ ə kwent) *adj.* pompous or high-flown in speech
Marcus gets *grandiloquent* when speaking of the theatre, assuming no one knows as much or has as refined a taste as he.
syn: pretentious *ant: plain-spoken*

10. **agrarian** (ə grâr´ ē ən) *adj.* concerning farms, farmers, or the use of land
    The economy of the *agrarian* nation depended on good crop yields.
    syn: agricultural *ant: urban; industrial*

11. **grimace** (grim´ is) *n.* a facial expression of fear, disapproval, or pain
    Amanda gave a *grimace* when Mrs. Hind assigned nine pages of algebra homework.
    syn: scowl *ant: smile*

12. **harangue** (hə rang´) *n.* a long, strongly expressed speech or lecture
    My wife delivered a lengthy *harangue* this morning in an effort to get me to quit smoking.
    syn: tirade

13. **formidable** (fôr´ mi də bəl) *adj.* arousing fear or awe
    When the hulking, 250-lb man stepped into the ring, Oscar knew that he had to face a *formidable* opponent.
    syn: intimidating

14. **sycophant** (sik´ ə fənt) n. a flatterer; one who fawns on others in order to gain favor
    Teri was such a *sycophant* that she laughed loudly at her supervisor's awful jokes.
    syn: toady *ant: contrarian*

15. **explicit** (ik splis´ ît) *adj.* clearly and openly stated; leaving nothing to the imagination
    Mom's instructions were *explicit*: Do not leave the house for any reason.
    syn: exact; precise *ant: ambiguous; vague*

EXERCISE I—Words in Context

From the list below, supply the words needed to complete the paragraph. Some words will not be used.

gadfly	**humility**	**arduous**	**affable**
grandiloquent	**harangue**	**grimace**	**sycophant**
explicit	**agrarian**		

A. "All the king's horses and all the king's men showed up tonight," mused Wyston to himself as he snatched another glass of champagne from the server's tray. He hated the governor's cocktail parties; it was always a[n] __________ task to maintain a friendly, __________ demeanor around so many obvious __________ seeking favors from the administration. After two hours, Wyston had to struggle to prevent his tired, polite smile from turning into a __________. It took all he had to pretend to listen and nod at the __________ stories of the wannabe rich and famous. There was also the annoying babble of the __________—single attendees who lacked the __________ required to be seen alone. They forced themselves into conversations and then held the listeners captive by withholding any opportunities to escape. When Wyston could no longer tolerate the pestering, he stepped outside and waited for the Governor to arrive and deliver his __________ to the idiotic crowd.

From the list below, supply the words needed to complete the paragraph. Some words will not be used.

humility	**dolorous**	**agrarian**	**gadfly**	**gargantuan**
avid	**explicit**	**formidable**	**epistle**	

B. The atmosphere at Aunt Agnes's farmhouse was __________ during the wake. No one could believe that Agnes was gone. At least, they reasoned, the __________ equestrian died while doing something that she loved. There was no definite explanation as to why Agnes's horse bucked her off, but by the looks of the __________ animal tracks, the horse had been spooked by a[n] __________ wolf, perhaps the largest ever seen.

The threat of wolves was nothing new to the __________ Van Ness family, who had been farming the northern valley for six generations. Wolves had attacked horses on the farm in the past, especially during extremely cold winters such as this one. Children on the farm always had __________ instructions to stay within sight of the house, but sometimes not even that was enough to protect the family from the hungry, silver predators.

Needing a break, Vicky wandered up the stairway to the second floor. Memories of her youth flashed through her head as she entered Agnes's room and sat on the corner of the bed. That's when she noticed the dusty corner of an old shoebox protruding from beneath the vanity. Curious, Vicky retrieved the box and, to her surprise, she found thirty years of hand-written __________, some of which were for Agnes, and some of which Agnes wrote but never sent.

EXERCISE II—Sentence Completion

Complete the sentence in a way that shows you understand the meaning of the italicized vocabulary word.

1. The summer help on the highway crew underestimated the *arduous* task of…
2. Through the smoke, I could tell by the *grimace* on Danforth's face that he…
3. Elliot could hardly tolerate the *grandiloquent* aristocrats while working at the…
4. To the dismay of the *sycophants*, the new foreman…
5. Jamie, the annoying *gadfly*, has a habit of…
6. The beach town published *explicit* rules about swimming after…
7. The arrogant stockbroker learned *humility* after…
8. In *agrarian* states, many young adults have extensive knowledge of…
9. The *gargantuan* Kodiak bear devoured…
10. Needing a break from her *dolorous* work as a coroner, Dr. Sinclair…
11. Unlike the fox, the bear turned out to be a *formidable* opponent because…
12. The history teacher's *harangue* this morning seemed to…
13. Mary Ellen's *avid* interest in chemistry led to her career as…
14. The senator's biography was actually a collection of *epistles* that…
15. The *affable* receptionist made everyone feel…

EXERCISE III—Roots, Prefixes, and Suffixes

Study the entries and answer the questions that follow.

The root *cosm* means "world" or "universe."
The root *cred* means "believe."
The suffixes *ic* and *id* mean "of" or "like."

A. *Using literal translations as guidance, define the following words without using a dictionary:*

1. cosmic	4. creed
2. cosmos	5. credentials
3. credible	6. credence

B. *Micro* means "small"; therefore, the word *microcosm* refers to a[n] __________ __________.

C. *Polites* means "citizen"; therefore, a *cosmopolitan* person is __________ ______________________.

D. List as many words as you can think of that contain the root *cred.*

EXERCISE IV—Inference

Complete the sentences by inferring information about the italicized word from its context.

A. If Kevin is no longer *affable* after his meeting with the manager, we might assume that the manager...

B. After the hard tackle during the championship game, the coach saw the *grimace* on Todd's face and knew...

C. Everyone knew that Bonnie was a *sycophant* because whenever the governor entered the room, Bonnie would...

EXERCISE V—Writing

Here is a writing prompt similar to the one you will find on the writing portion of the SAT.

Plan and write an essay based on the following statement:

> And then there were books, a kind of parallel universe
> in which anything might happen and frequently did,
> a universe in which I might be a newcomer but was
> never really a stranger. My real, true world.
>
> – Anna Quindlen
> *How Reading Changed My Life*
> The Ballantine Publishing Group, 1998

Assignment: Think of a book in which you felt you had discovered your real, true world. Write an essay describing how that is so. Use elements of plot, character, and setting to form your discussion.

Thesis: Write a *one-sentence* response to the above assignment. Make certain this single sentence offers a clear statement of your position.
Example: J.R.R. Tolkein's The Lord of the Rings *trilogy is sometimes more real to me than the world I live in because it inspires me to seek the inner hero in myself.*

Organizational Plan: If your thesis is the point on which you want to end, where does your essay need to begin? List the points of development that are inevitable in leading your reader from your beginning point to your end point. This list is your outline.

Draft: Use your thesis as both your beginning and your end. Following your outline, write a good first draft of your essay. Remember to support all your points with examples, facts, references to reading, etc.

Review and Revise: Exchange essays with a classmate. Using the scoring guide for Organization on page 206, score your partner's essay (while he or she scores yours). Focus on the organizational plan and use of language conventions. If necessary, rewrite your essay to improve the organizational plan and the use of language.

Improving Paragraphs

Read the following passage and then answer the multiple-choice questions that follow. Note that the questions will require you to make decisions regarding the revision of the reading selection.

D-Day

1 On November 8, 1942, American soldiers landed in North Africa. Fighting alongside the British Eighth Army, the Allies pushed the Germans out of North Africa. When the campaign was over, on May 12, 1943, the Allies had lost 70,000 men, while killing, wounding and capturing 350,000 Italian and German (Axis) soldiers. With North Africa taken, the Allies then invaded Italy. The plan was to drive up the boot of Italy, right into Germany, or so it seemed. Meanwhile, however, Allied plans were moving forward to invade the continent of Europe on the French coast.

2 The German generals, pessimistic at this point in the war, had good reason to be. They were pressed on the Eastern front by the Russians and in Italy by the Allies. Additionally, the German generals had an entire continent on which a third battlefront would surely be opened. Hitler and his generals knew that the pending Allied invasion would have to be crushed quickly. Only in this way could Hitler send more men to halt the Russian advance in the East. It was in this mood Hitler named General Rommel to be in charge of coastal defenses in France. While Hitler blamed Rommel for the defeats in North Africa, he also knew that Rommel was the most brilliant general he had.

3 When Rommel arrived, he was amazed at how little defensive work had been done. Throwing himself into his work, Rommel began construction on what he called the Atlantic Wall. This was to be a wall of coastal defenses that stretched from Norway to Spain. If Rommel had had the benefit of a few more months, some observers think he might have affected the outcome of the invasion. Another problem was the confusion in the German general staff. Because no one on the scene had complete authority, important things frequently did not get done. If Rommel had been in complete charge, some experts think that the Allied invasion would have been in greater trouble.

4 On June 6, 1944, the invasion began. More than 150,000 Allied troops landed on the beaches. They came ashore on the northern coast of France at Normandy. Their mission was to push Hitler's army back across the continent and completely crush the Nazi war machine. The soldiers were mostly from Britain, Canada, and the United States. The landing force had been preceded by 13,000 paratroopers who dropped behind the enemy's lines. The total invasion force was backed by the full force of Allied sea and air power. In the air, the Allies enjoyed a fifty-to-one advantage. On the ground they conducted the biggest amphibious assault ever attempted in modern warfare. Equipment for this landing had been stockpiled in the south of England in the months before the invasion. Code named "*Operation Overlord*," it was more popularly known as "D-Day." This attack proved to be the beginning of the end for Hitler and Nazi Germany.

5 U.S. General Dwight Eisenhower was the Supreme Commander of Allied forces based in Britain. He had the responsibility for leading the attack on the European continent. Eisenhower had described the military power that waited for D-Day as "a coiled spring." It was his responsibility to pick the day on which "this coiled spring" would let loose. In other words he must make the decision on when to launch the attack. This was an awesome responsibility, and the bad weather in the Channel made it a tough decision. There had already been two delays because of the weather. On June 6, however, Eisenhower gave the signal for the invasion to begin. The timing could not have been better. A brief break in the rainy weather that day allowed the ships to land the men and the tanks. In addition, Field Marshall Rommel had been convinced that the gale-force winds would continue. Knowing that the Allies had a history of waiting for clear weather, Rommel had decided that it was safe to return to Germany for his wife's birthday party. By the time he got back to the battlefront, the Allies were firmly dug in on French soil. The Allies had gotten a foothold on the continent, and they would not be turned back.

6 In planning the invasion, Eisenhower knew that fooling the enemy about the landing places was very important. In a brilliant plan of deception, Eisenhower had created a phony military unit called FUSAG or the First United States Army Group. Information was intentionally leaked to the Germans that this was the invading force that would land at Calais, France. Fake messages were sent, false troop locations were reported, and metal strips were dropped from planes to give the appearance of large air squadrons on German radar. This scheme was so convincing that Hitler was still waiting for the assault on Calais six weeks after the Allies landed at Normandy. The months following the assault on Normandy would see the Axis powers in full retreat on all fronts.

1. Which of the following would best improve the last two sentences of the first paragraph?
   A. Add, *it seemed,* after *plan*, put a semicolon after *Germany*, and delete *or so it seemed* and *Meanwhile.*
   B. Delete *however.*
   C. Delete *so it seemed* and combine the ideas into one sentence.
   D. Add *so it seemed* after *plan* and replace *Meanwhile, however,* with *But.*
   E. Delete both sentences.

2. How should paragraph 2 be edited to make it less confusing to the reader?
   A. Use *then* instead of *in this way* and delete *It was in this mood.*
   B. Delete the final paragraph.
   C. Replace *Only in this way* with *Only when crushed.*
   D. The paragraph is fine as it is.
   E. Replace *Only in this way* with *Only by stopping the Allies,* place a semicolon after *East*, and replace *It was in this mood* with *consequently*.

3. Paragraph 3 indicates *Another problem was the confusion.* Which of the following would best clarify what the initial problem was?
   A. Add a phrase to this sentence that begins, "the initial problem being..."
   B. Italicize the sentences that state the first problem.
   C. Explain again who General Rommel was.
   D. Change the word *problem* to *challenge.*
   E. Use the word *problem* earlier in the paragraph.

4. What should be done with the sentence in paragraph 5 that begins, *In other words* and ends with *attack?*
   A. Shorten it.
   B. Delete it.
   C. Lengthen it.
   D. Move it.
   E. Combine it with another sentence.

5. How could the last sentence of the essay be improved?
   A. Leave it as is.
   B. Reemphasize the success of the FUSAG ruse.
   C. Delete it entirely.
   D. Use it as the topic sentence of a new concluding paragraph.
   E. Combine it with the sentence immediately before it.

Lesson Twelve

1. **altercation** (ôl tər kā´ shən) *n.* a heated argument
   The mounting tension finally spawned an *altercation* between the police and the residents.
   syn: quarrel; dispute *ant: agreement; harmony*

2. **lexicon** (lek´ si kon´) *n.* a dictionary; a specialized vocabulary used in a particular field or place
   Having grown up in the inner city, Shawn was familiar with the *lexicon* of the streets.
   syn: jargon; argot; cant

3. **hue** (hyōō) *n.* a particular shade of a given color
   Dad was going to paint the shutters magenta, but Mom hates that *hue* and nixed the idea.

4. **galvanize** (gal´ və nīz) *v.* to startle into sudden activity
   A slight motion of the guard's rifle *galvanized* the lazy work crew into action.
   syn: stimulate *ant: enervate*

5. **sanction** (sangk´ shən) *n.* permission; support
   The teacher gave *sanction* to the student's odd but harmless habit of doing his homework in crayon.

6. **hyperbole** (hī pûr´ bə lē) *n.* extreme exaggeration for effect and not meant to be taken literally
   When Susan told her son she was going to kill him, it was only *hyperbole.*
   ant: understatement

7. **ominous** (om´ ə nəs) *adj.* threatening; foreboding evil
   We went on our picnic despite the *ominous* rain clouds.
   syn: sinister *ant: comforting*

8. **audacity** (ô das´ i tē) *n.* rude boldness; nerve
   Kate's father was enraged when she had the *audacity* to talk back to him.
   syn: insolence; impudence *ant: decorum*

9. **evince** (i vins´) *v.* to demonstrate clearly; to prove
   If you *evince* your theory, the university will fund your further studies.
   syn: manifest

10. **implacable** (im pla´ kə bəl) *adj.* unable to be appeased or pacified
Her *implacable* suspicions were finally put to rest when a private investigator assured her that her husband was faithful.
syn: inflexible; relentless *ant: pacified; assuaged*

11. **exhort** (ig zôrt´) *v.* to urge on with stirring words
During halftime, the coach *exhorted* his team to "win one for the Gipper."
syn: encourage

12. **incarcerate** (in kär´ sə rāt) *v.* to put into prison; to confine
We were shocked that the police *incarcerated* Rafael for something as minor as stealing hubcaps.
syn: imprison; constrain *ant: liberate; free*

13. **incisive** (in sī´ siv) *adj.* sharp; keen; cutting straight to the heart of the matter
I had thought the meeting would run for hours, but Sharon made a few *incisive* comments that settled matters without wasting time or words.
syn: piercing; acute *ant: superficial; dull*

14. **expedient** (ik spē´ dē ənt) *adj.* practical; providing an immediate advantage (especially when serving one's self-interest)
Lying, while not admirable, did prove to be the most *expedient* way to obtain the information.
syn: effective *ant: feckless*

15. **pertinent** (pûr´ tn ənt) *adj.* having to do with the subject at hand; relevant
The lecturer took questions as long as they were *pertinent* and enriched the discussion.
ant: unrelated; extraneous

EXERCISE I—Words in Context

From the list below, supply the words needed to complete the paragraph. Some words will not be used.

ominous	**exhort**	**galvanize**	**hyperbole**
expedient	**implacable**	**incisive**	**hue**

A. "What are you doing, you guys? I shouldn't have to __________ you at this point in the game!" __________ by Liza's scream, the four workers picked up their sanders and returned to their unfinished portions of drywall.

"We're two days overdue! That means we're paying them now!" The worker closest to Liza turned a[n] __________ of red as she screamed. He knew that Liza's lecture was not merely __________ to get the team to work faster; the contractors really were beyond their deadline. Liza was worried for good reason; if the company couldn't prove that it was capable of __________, short-notice refurbishing, it would more than likely lose its contract with the city.

Myron, the site foreman, appreciated Liza's __________ comments. At least she took the time to explain why the workers needed to labor more quickly. Such practice reminded the workers of just how small the degree of separation was between the company's success and their paychecks. It also prevented the workers from classifying Liza as a[n] __________ manager who just wanted to make a profit. If the workers knew that the company was suffering, they knew that their jobs were in jeopardy.

From the list below, supply the words needed to complete the paragraph. Some words will not be used.

altercation	**lexicon**	**sanction**	**ominous**
audacity	**evince**	**incarcerate**	**pertinent**
implacable	**galvanize**		

B. Eugene had worked at the genetics lab for six days when he witnessed the noisy __________ between Dr. Strangeon and his research assistant. "You know that I didn't __________ an early run of the Beta-Gen module! Now you've destroyed the entire lot!" Strangeon was definitely irate, and Eugene wished that he understood more of the laboratory __________ that the doctor spouted at his assistant.

"How could you—you're not an intern anymore—how could you have the __________ to go off on your own and initiate a test run of a model that required eight years of research and over twelve million dollars to develop? Well?" The assistant could only mutter an answer.

"I just thought—I—uh—I wanted to see if—"

"What you want is not __________ here!" shouted the doctor. "You've only managed to __________ the fact that you're unfit to work in a laboratory! We should press charges and have the police __________ you! Now get out!"

The problem, thought Eugene, probably involved whatever Dr. Strangeon stored behind the __________ pair of tall, armored doors with the retina-scanning lock mechanism. Dr. Strangeon and his assistant had been the only two people to enter that room during the week that Eugene had been employed at the lab.

EXERCISE II—Sentence Completion

Complete the sentence in a way that shows you understand the meaning of the italicized vocabulary word.

1. The *ominous* gates in front of the old mansion made us...
2. Lonnie's face turned a *hue* of green after...
3. Be sure to get *sanction* before you try to enter the...
4. The *incisive* instructions made it easy for Lynn to...
5. The *expedient* dam of sandbags prevented the floodwaters from...
6. *Galvanized* by the sound of the screaming foreman, the workers...
7. In the courtroom, the prisoner had the *audacity* to...
8. I don't need to *evince* my value at this company because...
9. During the peace talks, the *implacable* general refused...
10. The physical *altercation* between the brothers caused the neighbors to...
11. The sergeant was advised to *exhort* the platoon prior to the...
12. To master the *lexicon* of the law, John...
13. It seemed *hyperbole* to me when my teacher said...
14. The paramedics wanted only *pertinent* information because...
15. The judge decided to *incarcerate* Tara because...

EXERCISE III—Roots, Prefixes, and Suffixes

Study the entries and answer the questions that follow.

The root *dorm* means "sleep."
The root *fin* means "end."
The suffix *ory* means "a place for."
The root *nom* means "name."
The suffix *ee* means "one who is."
The prefix *in* means "not."
The root *clat* means "calling" or "system of calling."

A. *Using literal translations as guidance, define the following words without using a dictionary:*

1. dormitory
2. dormant
3. nominee
4. nomenclature
5. finale
6. infinite

B. You might see the grand finale at the __________ of a show.

C. Since the mayor-for-a-day position was only *nominal*, Colette could not
____.

D. List as many words as you can think of that contain the roots *dorm, fin,* and *nom.*

EXERCISE IV—Inference

Complete the sentences by inferring information about the italicized word from its context.

A. If you don't have *sanction* to sell refreshments in the stadium, the security guards might...

B. Mr. Moulan's *expedient* methods to get rich were probably to blame for...

C. Judging by the debris on the highway and the intensity of the drivers' *altercation*, I assumed that the two drivers...

EXERCISE V—Critical Reading

Below is a pair of reading passages followed by several multiple-choice questions similar to the ones you will encounter on the SAT. Carefully read both passages and choose the best answer to each of the questions.

The two passages offer contrasting views of autumn and the implications of the change of seasons.

Passage 1

1 Autumn is the third season of the year, and it brings us many gifts as the earth passes the prime of its year. This period between summer and winter is a time when deciduous foliage returns itself to the earth for rejuvenation, even though rejuvenation is probably the last term that we would use to describe the sight of our favorite shade trees, shrubs, and scented blossoms denuding themselves.

2 Deciduous plants and trees slowly lose the chlorophyll in their leaves as the weather changes from balmy summer days to frosty mornings and chilly evenings. The sun sets earlier, and the trees and plants lose the energy they need to maintain the green color in their leaves. Leaves turn to gorgeous yellows and flaming reds and, after an exquisite show, they depart from their branches and fall back to the earth, signaling that the preparation for rebirth has begun.

3 The blanket of fallen leaves conceals a very special event. Nature is pregnant, and in six months, the offspring of every tree, plant, shrub, and flower will begin new lives as budding leaves or shoots from acorns. A bank of majestic proportion, the autumn earth will have reclaimed its green lives on loan and placed them in a high interest account for the duration of winter. Upon spring, the investment matures, and the earth overflows with more life than the previous year.

4 The deposits of each species vary in size, and each species has its own method of reclaiming its capital when spring arrives. Trees reclaim their large leaf currency, and spindly branches, leafless the previous year, produce shoots that will soon flower. Brush thrives on the nourishment of the soil in which it grows, now rich from the decomposed leaves from the previous autumn.

5 The prologue to the annual renaissance should be admired and enjoyed, for it is a privilege to witness such an epic natural event. Knowing that new life is in the making beneath the barren limbs and snow covered fields might create a little more warmth during a long, frigid winter.

Passage 2

1 Each year, around September, fall arrives just in time to ruin the summer. The name of this season—fall—is ironic because it also describe our mental process upon its arrival. We fall. We fall in spirit as the days grow short and we are further confined to our homes. We fall in health because influenza season begins. Our ambition falls, and with it goes productivity. In general, we fall apart.

2 Fall brings nothing good except football, and that doesn't even last long. It is depressing to watch as the fun activities of summer drift away, particularly trips to the beach, volleyball games, baseball, and camping excursions. We cannot take them inside, but we can't continue them because the weather is just too cold.

3 Centers of activity close after Labor Day, and we might as well lock ourselves inside and do what bears do in the winter: hibernate. People, like animals, have no reason to be outdoors in the winter. The world beyond the front porch grows dark, devoid of the bright colors of summer clothes, red convertibles, flowers, and beach umbrellas.

4 Even nature closes shop in the fall. Leaves drop from tree limbs, and plants wither to their roots, leaving a barren, brown landscape in place of what was a picturesque Rockwell painting. The only green objects left are holly bushes and fir trees, neither of which can be touched without getting pricked by their needles. Crickets cease to chirp, and the lights of fireflies burn out. The only insects that remain are the type that want to enter our homes to stay warm. Even the birds know better than to stick around; flocks of geese steer themselves southward, happily honking their retreat from misery.

5 Fall is the worst time of the year because the most beautiful parts of nature die. Gloomy, forbidding desolation shrouds the world, assisted by the waning sun, the silence of the wind passing through barren forests, and the stink of rotting leaves. Nature is dead; we would do best to remain in our caves (or homes) until the long and intolerable season passes.

1. The mood of the first passage could best be described as
   A. jovial.
   B. sad.
   C. expectant.
   D. optimistic.
   E. enthusiastic.

2. What is the closest definition of the word *deciduous* as used in paragraph 2?
   A. indecisive
   B. shedding leaves annually
   C. colorful
   D. green all year
   E. temporary

3. What does the author mean by using the metaphor of a bank in paragraph 3, passage 1?
   A. Everything here is on loan.
   B. Deposits earn interest.
   C. Spring borrows from autumn.
   D. The earth is the holder of all assets.
   E. The universe is bigger than just the earth.

4. In the first passage, the probable intention of paragraphs 3 and 4 is
   A. to make fun of autumn.
   B. to make the reader aware of nature.
   C. to point out the differences among leaves.
   D. to compare the colors of spring and autumn.
   E. to create a positive, expectant mood.

5. What is the justification for the author's comparison of autumn and a human pregnancy?
   A. to imply the earth can regenerate itself as humans can
   B. to take the reader's mind off seasonal problems
   C. to provide evidence that autumn is the most important season
   D. to provide a relationship between the reader and autumn
   E. to give purpose to an otherwise dismal time of year

6. How would you define the word *fall* in the context of the second passage?
   A. Fall means to drop from a tree.
   B. Fall means everything falls down dead.
   C. Fall means a decline in natural growth and human activity.
   D. Fall means a similarity to a hank of false hair.
   E. Fall means to be disappointed.

7. Why does the author think that people should do the same as bears?
   A. No picnic sites are open after Labor Day.
   B. Darkness comes earlier in the fall.
   C. After Labor Day, all worthwhile activity ends.
   D. Protective coats are available by waiting.
   E. Nothing constructive can be accomplished in the fall.

8. What is the predominant emotion of the second passage?
   A. hopefulness
   B. despair
   C. anger
   D. disappointment
   E. anticipation

9. Which of the following best sums up the second-passage author's attitude toward fall?
   A. It will be a long time before next spring comes.
   B. The death of flowers is the worst part of fall.
   C. Fall represents an inevitable stage in the cycle of life.
   D. Though depressing on the surface, fall provides an affirming optimism.
   E. Fall is aptly named because everything "goes down" during the season.

10. Which of the following best pinpoints the similarity between the two passages?
    A. Each passage has a great deal of factual description.
    B. Each passage tells a story about a season.
    C. Each passage creates a mood.
    D. Each passage presents a case for its own cause.
    E. Each passage informs without consideration of emotion.

11. What is the major difference between the two passages?
    A. The first passage has more pertinent information than the second, which doesn't supply enough facts.
    B. The second passage relies on negativity to create its mood, while the first passage brings out all other points.
    C. The first passage does not emphasize summer or lost pleasures; the second passage dwells on the passing of summer.
    D. The second passage is shorter than the first and takes less time to read.
    E. The less joyful of the two passages is placed below the first to create a negative impression.

12. Which of the following would be the best appraisal of the two passages?
    A. We have to take the good with the bad.
    B. Even this we will one day look on as pleasant.
    C. We always have something to look forward to.
    D. Nothing is all bad, not even fall.
    E. There are two sides to every story.

Lesson Thirteen

1. **inert** (in ûrt´) *adj.* unable to act or move; inactive; sluggish
   All dangerous components have been removed from the *inert* missile on display at the science museum.
   syn: dormant; passive *ant: dynamic; active*

2. **circumvent** (sûr kəm vent´) *v.* to get around; to bypass
   Though she did not lie, the defendant *circumvented* the question by claiming she could not remember where she was at the time.
   syn: avoid

3. **clandestine** (klan des´ tin) *adj.* secret
   Romeo and Juliet were forced to hold *clandestine* meetings because of their parents' feuding.
   syn: covert; furtive *ant: open; aboveboard*

4. **acquit** (ə kwit´) *v.* to find not guilty of a fault or crime
   The jury *acquitted* the man, and he was free to go.
   syn: absolve *ant: convict*

5. **deprecate** (dep´ ri kāt) *v.* to express strong disapproval of
   Doug stopped offering new ideas after the other workers *deprecated* his first suggestion.
   syn: deplore *ant: approve; praise*

6. **barrister** (bar´ i stər) *n.* lawyer (British)
   The *barrister* questioned the witness as to his familiarity with a certain London pub.

7. **adulation** (aj ōō lā´ shən) *n.* excessive praise or admiration
   Kim despised the *adulation* heaped on rock stars by young fans.
   syn: flattery; adoration *ant: derision*

8. **culinary** (kul´ ə ner ē) *adj.* having to do with the kitchen or cooking
   The famous chef had been a life-long student of the *culinary* arts.

9. **bawdy** (bô´ dē) *adj.* indecent; humorously obscene
   When some called the new sitcom *bawdy*, the toy company quickly withdrew its sponsorship.
   syn: risqué; lewd *ant: innocent; clean*

10. **chastise** (chas tīz´) *v.* to punish severely
    Brother Jacques *chastised* Archie for skipping Latin by grounding him for the semester.
    syn: discipline

11. **jocose** (jō kōs´) *adj.* joking; humorous
    Gary's *jocose* manner often led people to say he should become a stand-up comedian.
    syn: witty; funny; playful; jocund *ant: serious*

12. **myriad** (mir´ ē əd) *n.* a very large number
    adj. too numerous to be counted
    (n.) After my break-up, my mom fed me the old line about there being a *myriad* of fish in the sea.
    (a.) The biologist spent her entire career categorizing the *myriad* plant species of the rain forest.
    (n.) *syn: host; multitude*
    (a.) *syn: countless; innumerable* *ant: few; limited*

13. **latent** (lāt´ nt) *adj.* present, but not active; hidden
    After retiring, Nat took up painting and found that he had had *latent* artistic talents all along.
    syn: dormant *ant: manifest*

14. **pernicious** (pər nish´ əs) *adj.* destructive; deadly
    The *pernicious* plague wiped out half the country's population.
    syn: malignant; harmful *ant: benign*

15. **frugal** (frōō´ gəl) *adj.* thrifty; economical in money matters
    My *frugal* father buys only day-old bread and marked-down fruit.
    syn: economical *ant: wasteful; profligate*

EXERCISE I—Words in Context

From the list below, supply the words needed to complete the paragraph. Some words will not be used.

culinary	**pernicious**	**latent**	**frugal**	**circumvent**
clandestine	**inert**	**jocose**	**myriad**	

A. Like a[n] __________ saboteur hiding in enemy territory waiting for the go-ahead signal, the tiny microorganism infiltrated the deepest, most vulnerable parts of its host and remained in a dormant state. Waves of red blood cells knocked the __________ bacterium about, tossing its __________, suspended form from one membrane to the next. The germ waited, as it had for days, until the host's chemistry was perfect for waking from its slumber and unleashing its __________ toll on the host's body.

In a few hours, the single microbe would multiply into a __________, and then the tiny legion would seize control of the host's nervous system. Not even the best research scientists could find a way to __________ the deadly effects of the microscopic villains.

From the list below, supply the words needed to complete the paragraph. Some words will not be used.

adulation	**frugal**	**acquit**	**myriad**
jocose	**barrister**	**chastise**	**deprecate**

B. "What are you being so __________ about? We're in a courtroom, you fool; shut up."

Scolded by his only friend in the room, Giles stopped laughing but maintained his crooked smirk. His __________ was quickly losing patience; both he and Giles knew that there was no chance that the judge was going to __________ him. This was his second appearance before Justice Quentin, and by the way in which the judge __________ Giles during the previous trial, he knew that he wasn't going to get away this time. As the smirk faded, Giles wished that he hadn't been so __________ while shopping for lawyers.

From the list below, supply the words needed to complete the paragraph. Some words will not be used.

frugal **bawdy** **adulation** **clandestine** **deprecate** **culinary**

C. Theme restaurants do not usually become popular for the quality of their cuisine, but the Gold Mine, operated in the likeness of a California gold-rush saloon, has received the __________ of every food critic who ate there. The saloon is one of few tourism-dependent restaurants that gives as much attention to its __________ performance as to the nightly stage shows featuring vaudeville-style comedians, singers, and cancan dancers wearing the __________ saloon outfits of the period. After twenty years of service, few patrons—if any—have been able to __________ the quality of food and entertainment at the Gold Mine.

EXERCISE II—Sentence Completion

Complete the sentence in a way that shows you understand the meaning of the italicized vocabulary word.

1. Paul was *acquitted* of the crime, but the general public still believed...
2. My *bawdy* uncle really didn't fit in at the...
3. As the fallen disco ball struck the floor, a *myriad* of...
4. Derek was so *frugal* that he refused to...
5. To sneak the missile data out of the compound, the *clandestine* operator...
6. The *barrister* feared his client's associates after...
7. The *latent* saboteur waited for the signal to...
8. The swarm of *pernicious* locusts caused the farmer to...
9. No one thought that it was too extreme to *chastise* Gary for...
10. The crowd's *adulation* for Monique revealed her...
11. When you finish using the *culinary* utensils, please...
12. Some people laugh at Ken, but others find his *jocose* manner to be...
13. Feel free to *deprecate* my idea now, but not when we're in front of...
14. The *inert* Jose lay on the couch after an exhausting day of...
15. To *circumvent* the broken power line, the electric company...

EXERCISE III—Roots, Prefixes, and Suffixes

Study the entries and answer the questions that follow.

The roots *fac, fact, fect,* and *fic* mean "make" or "do."
The root *grat* means "please."
The suffix *tude* means "the state of."
The roots *mot* and *mov* mean "to move."
The prefix *con* means "with."
The prefix *re* means "away."
The prefix *de* means "down."

A. *Using literal translations as guidance, define the following words without using a dictionary:*

1. factory
2. gratitude
3. congratulations
4. motivation
5. remote
6. demote

B. A person who does certain activities very well can be said to have a ___________________ for them.
If you ease the progress of a class meeting, you could be called a[n] ___________________.

C. If you are feeling thankful for someone's help, you might describe your feeling as ___________________.

D. List as many words as you can think of that contain the roots *fac, fact, fect, fic,* or *grat.*

EXERCISE IV—Inference

Complete the sentences by inferring information about the italicized word from its context.

A. If the foreman usually *deprecates* the behavior of his employees, the workers will probably…

B. If Eddie's parents *chastise* him by taking away his car keys, you might assume that Eddie…

C. When a *myriad* of sparks emerged from beneath her car, Lanna was glad that she…

EXERCISE V—Writing

Here is a writing prompt similar to the one you will find on the writing portion of the SAT.

Plan and write an essay based on the following statement:

> It was a high counsel that I once heard given to a young person, "Always do what you are afraid to do."
> – Ralph Waldo Emerson

Assignment: Write an essay in which you support or refute the above statement. Be certain to support your claim with evidence from literature, the arts, science and technology, current events, or your experience or observation.

Thesis: Write a one-sentence response to the above assignment. Make certain this single sentence offers a clear statement of your position.
Example: A person might accomplish great deeds, but never will if prevented by fear of failure.

Organizational Plan: If your thesis is the point on which you want to end, where does your essay need to begin? List the points of development that are inevitable in leading your reader from your beginning point to your end point. This list is your outline.

Draft: Use your thesis as both your beginning and your end. Following your outline, write a good first draft of your essay. Remember to support all your points with examples, facts, references to reading, etc.

Review and Revise: Exchange essays with a classmate. Using the scoring guide for Development on page 207, score your partner's essay (while he or she scores yours). Focus on the development of ideas and use of language conventions. If necessary, rewrite your essay to improve the development and the use of language.

Identifying Sentence Errors

Identify the grammatical errors in the following sentences. If the sentence contains no error, select answer E.

1. When I met (A) my uncle, I was shocked (B) to see that (C) he doesn't have hardly (D) any hair. No error (E)

2. When my mother (A) went to do (B) the shopping, I would of cleaned (C) my room, but I fell asleep (D) No error (E)

3. The stationery part (A) of the clock is in the center, (B) but the outer edge rotates (C) with every passing (D) second. No error (E)

4. My father said I could (A) associate with whoever (B) I wanted, as long as I didn't bring (C) anyone home for dinner (D). No error (E)

5. Any woman (A) who doesn't meet the necessary requirements will (B) have their name (C) removed from the list (D) of candidates. No error (E)

Improving Sentences

The underlined portion of each sentence contains some flaw. Select the answer that best corrects the flaw.

6. Sleeping peacefully, we finally located the lost puppy in an abandoned mine tunnel.
   A. Sleeping peacefully, we located the puppy finally in an abandoned mine tunnel.
   B. In an abandoned mine tunnel, we finally located the lost puppy sleeping peacefully.
   C. We finally located the lost puppy sleeping peacefully in an abandoned mine tunnel.
   D. Finally in an abandoned mine tunnel we found sleeping peacefully the lost puppy.
   E. We located the puppy lost in an abandoned mine tunnel finally sleeping peacefully.

7. The coach, along with the managers and team members, were praised during the varsity sports banquet.
   A. were praised for their performance during the varsity sports banquet.
   B. was praised during the varsity sports banquet.
   C. was praised for their performance during the varsity sports banquet.
   D. were praised during the Varsity Sports Banquet.
   E. was praised for their performance during the season.

8. Our outdoor party quickly went inside when news of the approaching tornado was received by us.
   A. When our outdoor party went inside, we quickly heard news of an approaching tornado.
   B. When we quickly went inside, our outdoor party news was an approaching tornado.
   C. An approaching tornado was news when our outdoor party went inside quickly.
   D. Our outdoor party, when news of an approaching tornado went quickly, we went inside.
   E. When we received news of an approaching tornado, our outdoor party quickly went inside.

9. A suitcase was seen floating on Milltown Creek, but no one knew who's it was.
   A. A suitcase was seen floating on Milltown Creek, but no one knew whose it was.
   B. No one knew who's suitcase was seen on Milltown Creek floating.
   C. Floating on Milltown Creek was seen a suitcase, but no one knew who's it was.
   D. Milltown Creek was seen with a floating suitcase, but no one knew who's it was.
   E. Who's suitcase was seen floating on Milltown Creek?

10. Finding a bag of sandwiches in the bank vault, while the police were investigating a bank robbery.
   A. A bag of sandwiches in the bank vault while police were investigating a bank robbery were found.
   B. In the bank vault, police investigating a bank robbery, finding a bag of sandwiches.
   C. While investigating a bag of sandwiches, police were found in the bank vault robbery.
   D. While investigating a bank robbery, police found a bag of sandwiches in the bank vault.
   E. The bank vault, a bag of sandwiches, and the police in a robbery investigation.

Lesson Fourteen

1. **levity** (lev´ i tē) *n.* lightness of disposition; lack of seriousness
   Kent brought an air of *levity* to the otherwise somber proceedings by cracking a few jokes.
   syn: frivolity *ant: sobriety; somberness*

2. **hoax** (hōks) *n.* a practical joke; a trick
   The sighting of Elvis at the Bowl-O-Rama turned out to be a *hoax.*
   syn: fraud; fake

3. **amicable** (am´ i kə bəl) *adj.* friendly; peaceable
   Commerce will suffer until the two nations establish *amicable* relations.
   syn: agreeable; amiable *ant: quarrelsome; warlike*

4. **obstreperous** (ob strep´ ər əs) *adj.* aggressively boisterous; stubborn and defiant
   The *obstreperous* mob of looters was finally subdued by an icy blast from the fire hose.
   ant: meek; tractable

5. **enraptured** (en rap´ chərd) *adj.* delighted beyond measure
   Sasha was *enraptured* by the performance of the visiting ballet troupe.
   syn: ecstatic

6. **marital** (mar´ i təl) *adj.* having to do with marriage
   Marital problems can sometimes be solved by a session with a marriage counselor.
   syn: wedded *ant: single*

7. **bask** (bask) *v.* to expose oneself to pleasant warmth
   During the Florida vacation, all she did was *bask* in the sun.

8. **genial** (jēn´ yəl) *adj.* friendly; amiable
   Our new neighbors were so *genial* that we felt we had known them for years.
   syn: cordial *ant: unfriendly*

9. **charlatan** (shär´ lə ten) *n.* one who pretends to have knowledge in order to swindle others
   The supposed doctor endorsing the fat-burning "miracle drug" was actually a *charlatan.*
   syn: quack; fraud *ant: professional*

10. **mundane** (mun dān´) *adj.* commonplace; earthly and not spiritual
Virginia thought herself too good an artist to be expected to deal with *mundane* things like earning a living.
syn: boring *ant: unique*

11. **fickle** (fik´ əl) *adj.* likely to change on a whim or without apparent reason
Because she never kept one boyfriend for long, her friends said Keisha was *fickle.*
syn: vacillating; capricious *ant: steadfast*

12. **juggernaut** (jug´ ər nôt) *n.* a terrible destructive or irresistible force
The Nazi *juggernaut* swept through Belgium and into France.

13. **naïve** (nä ēv´) *adj.* simple in outlook; not affected or worldly; especially innocent
Old movies usually portray country girls in the city as *naïve* and vulnerable.
syn: unsophisticated; unsuspecting *ant: sophisticated; cunning*

14. **nocturnal** (nok tûr´ nəl) *adj.* having to do with the night; occurring at night
Owls are *nocturnal* creatures; they sleep during the day.
ant: diurnal

15. **novice** (nov´ is) *n.* a beginner; one who is inexperienced
The older lawyer took the *novice* under her wing and showed him the ropes.
syn: apprentice; tyro *ant: master*

EXERCISE I—Words in Context

From the list below, supply the words needed to complete the paragraph. Some words will not be used.

charlatan	**naïve**	**enraptured**	**hoax**	**amicable**
levity	**bask**	**fickle**	**mundane**	

A. When the __________ citizens of Reynoldsville finally realized that their forty-cent bottles of miracle sap contained nothing more than licorice extract and whiskey, they formed a lynch mob and searched for the __________ who had sold the fake elixir. Fortunately, Colonel Britton, the quack they were looking for, had already taken his wagon and quietly left town before dawn. He rode nonstop for a full day until, in his usual routine, he pulled far off the trail and spent a day restocking his miracle sap, occasionally breaking to partake of some himself. __________ by the beautiful scenery of the Black Hills, Britton didn't waste his opportunity to __________ in the low autumn sun for the remainder of the afternoon. While most of his clientele were desensitized to the beauty of nature after spending harsh lives in it, Britton never once considered his private outings to be __________; if he didn't spend at least a few hours enjoying nature every week, he had trouble maintaining his __________ demeanor whenever he rolled into a new town. If Britton didn't at least appear to be happy, people were not going to purchase his tonic, whether it was a[n] __________ or not. His customers were very __________ about spending their money; if they had even the slightest notion that Britton's product was a scam, they would not buy it.

From the list below, supply the words needed to complete the paragraph. Some words will not be used.

genial	**enraptured**	**nocturnal**	**obstreperous**
novice	**juggernaut**	**marital**	**levity**

B. Despite her position as regional manager for Tyndall Systems, Shawna felt like a[n] __________ every time she attended the monthly sales meeting at Tyndall corporate headquarters. Perhaps she was just getting old, she reasoned, but she knew that few could endure her nearly __________ schedule of working late into the night on six days out of the week. Tyndall was a[n] __________ in the information technology arena, buying and consolidating other corporations and firing dissenters with impunity. Shawna told her husband that she would retire in two years, she hoped in time to mitigate their rapidly multiplying __________ problems. She was no longer the hard worker that Tyndall wanted for managing a regional hub, and the stress from trying to meet the demand had caused her once __________ manner to reverse—not that she needed it any more at the office. District sales meetings were not a place for __________; the twelve other managers spoke and carried themselves like assertive robots, rarely allowing jokes or laughter to interrupt their lengthy meetings. The single and most recent show of emotion at the meeting occurred when the vice president fired one of the managers on the spot, and the security guards had to drag him, __________ and screaming, out of the conference room.

EXERCISE II—Sentence Completion

Complete the sentence in a way that shows you understand the meaning of the italicized vocabulary word.

1. When the ambulance pulled up, everyone knew that Kristen's *hoax* had…
2. The *juggernaut* of tanks rolled effortlessly through…
3. The Clarks revealed few *marital* problems, but I knew that…
4. Katie *basked* in the bright August sun until she…
5. The *naïve* young soldier had difficulty accepting…
6. The *nocturnal* raccoons waited until the camping family was asleep before …
7. The zookeepers struggled to move the *obstreperous* lion to…
8. The *fickle* customers will not return to the store if…
9. Our *genial* neighbor always invites us…
10. Your *levity* in the present situation is…
11. No one ever would have guessed that the *charlatan* was not really a…
12. Mount Everest is not a place for *novice*…

13. The job might be *mundane*, but the city is...

14. Instead of attacking, the *amicable* natives...

15. Jules, an amateur chef, was *enraptured* by the master chef's invitation to...

EXERCISE III—Roots, Prefixes, and Suffixes

Study the entries, and answer the questions that follow.

The root *hydr* means "water."
The root *junct* means "join."
The suffix *phobia* means "fear of."
The prefix *de* means "down," "away from," "about."
The prefixes *dis, di,* and *dif* mean "apart" or "not."
The prefix *con* means "with."

A. *Using literal translations as guidance, define the following words without using a dictionary:*

1. dehydration
2. hydrophobia
3. disjointed
4. conjunction
5. juncture
6. hydroelectric

B. *Hydraulics* is the branch of physics that deals with ________________ ________________________.

C. *Therm* is a root which means "heat"; therefore, *hydrothermal* has to do with ____.

D. List as many words as you can think of that contain the roots *hydr* and *junct.*

EXERCISE IV—Inference

Complete the sentences by inferring information about the italicized word from its context.

A. If the police determine that the suspicious package is a *hoax*, then it is probably safe for the evacuated employees to...

B. All the drivers waiting on the highway honked their horns because the farmer couldn't get the *obstreperous*...

C. If people respond to Myra's *levity* with angry glares, it is because she shouldn't be...

EXERCISE V—Critical Reading

Below is a reading passage followed by several multiple-choice questions similar to the ones you will encounter on the SAT. Carefully read the passage and choose the best answer to each of the questions.

The following is an excerpt from Mark Twain's satirical essay, "On the Decay of the Art of Lying." Twain discusses the types of truth that people do—and do not—want to hear.

Observe, I do not mean to suggest that the *custom* of lying has suffered any decay or interruption—no, for the Lie, as a Virtue, a Principle, is eternal; the Lie, as a recreation, a solace, a refuge in time of need, the fourth Grace, the tenth Muse, man's best and surest friend, is immortal,
(5) and cannot perish from the earth while this club remains. My complaint simply concerns the decay of the *art* of lying. No high-minded man, no man of right feeling, can contemplate the lumbering and slovenly lying of the present day without grieving to see a noble art so prostituted. In this veteran presence I naturally enter upon this theme with diffidence;
(10) it is like an old maid trying to teach nursery matters to the mothers in Israel. It would not become to me to criticize you, gentlemen—who are nearly all my elders—and my superiors, in this thing—if I should here and there *seem* to do it, I trust it will in most cases be more in a spirit of admiration than fault-finding; indeed if this finest of the fine
(15) arts had everywhere received the attention, the encouragement, and conscientious practice and development which this club has devoted to it, I should not need to utter this lament, or shed a single tear. I do not say this to flatter: I say it in a spirit of just and appreciative recognition. [It had been my intention, at this point, to mention names and to give
(20) illustrative specimens, but indications observable about me admonished

me to beware of the particulars and confine myself to generalities.]

No fact is more firmly established than that lying is a necessity of our circumstances—the deduction that it is then a Virtue goes without saying. No virtue can reach its highest usefulness without careful and diligent cultivation—therefore, it goes without saying that this one ought to be taught in the public schools—even in the newspapers. What chance has the ignorant uncultivated liar against the educated expert? What chance have I against Mr. Per—against a lawyer? *Judicious* lying is what the world needs. I sometimes think it were even better and safer not to lie at all than to lie injudiciously. An awkward, unscientific lie is often as ineffectual as the truth.

Now let us see what the philosophers say. Note that venerable proverb: Children and fools *always* speak the truth. The deduction is plain—adults and wise persons *never* speak it. Parkman, the historian, says, "The principle of truth may itself be carried into an absurdity." In another place in the same chapters he says, "The saying is old that truth should not be spoken at all times; and those whom a sick conscience worries into habitual violation of the maxim are imbeciles and nuisances." It is strong language, but true. None of us could *live* with an habitual truth-teller; but thank goodness none of us has to. An habitual truth-teller is simply an impossible creature; he does not exist; he never has existed. Of course there are people who *think* they never lie, but it is not so—and this ignorance is one of the very things that shame our so-called civilization. Everybody lies—every day; every hour; awake; asleep; in his dreams; in his joy; in his mourning; if he keeps his tongue still, his hands, his feet, his eyes, his attitude, will convey deception—and purposely. Even in sermons—but that is a platitude.

In a far country where I once lived the ladies used to go around paying calls, under the humane and kindly pretence of wanting to see each other; and when they returned home, they would cry out with a glad voice, saying, "We made sixteen calls and found fourteen of them out"—not meaning that they found out anything important against the fourteen—no, that was only a colloquial phrase to signify that they were not at home—and their manner of saying it expressed their lively satisfaction in that fact. Now their pretence of wanting to see the fourteen—and the other two whom they had been less lucky with—was that commonest and mildest form of lying which is sufficiently described as a deflection from the truth. Is it justifiable? Most certainly. It is beautiful, it is noble; for its object is, *not* to reap profit, but to convey a pleasure to the sixteen. The iron-souled truth monger would plainly manifest, or even utter the fact that he didn't want to see those people—and he would be an ass, and inflict totally unnecessary pain. And next, those ladies in that far country—but never mind, they had a thousand pleasant ways of lying, that grew out of gentle impulses, and were a credit to their intelligence and an honor to their hearts. Let the particulars go.

The men in that far country were liars, every one. Their mere howdy-do was a lie, because *they* didn't care how you did, except they were undertakers. To the ordinary inquirer you lied in return; for you made

no conscientious diagnostic of your case, but answered at random, and
70 usually missed it considerably. You lied to the undertaker, and said your health was failing—a wholly commendable lie, since it cost you nothing and pleased the other man. If a stranger called and interrupted you, you said with your hearty tongue, "I'm glad to see you," and said with your heartier soul, "I wish you were with the cannibals and it was dinner-
75 time." When he went, you said regretfully, "*Must* you go?" and followed it with a "Call again;" but you did no harm, for you did not deceive anybody nor inflict any hurt, whereas the truth would have made you both unhappy....

Joking aside, I think there is much need of wise examination into
80 what sorts of lies are best and wholesomest to be indulged, seeing we *must* all lie and we *do* all lie, and what sorts it may be best to avoid—and this is a thing which I feel I can confidently put into the hands of this experienced Club—a ripe body, who may be termed, in this regard, and without undue flattery, Old Masters.

1. The purpose of the personification in line 4 is to
   A. express the decline of lying.
   B. emphasize that the custom of lying is improving.
   C. suggest how lying is embedded in human nature.
   D. propose a movement toward universal truth.
   E. point out the inconveniences that lying can cause.

2. The "far country" mentioned in paragraphs 4 and 5 most likely refers to
   A. Twain's contemporary society.
   B. Twain's visit to Italy in the 1850s.
   C. the customs of earlier times.
   D. the way Twain feels society should be.
   E. the customs of the American West.

3. Based on the context, what is the most accurate meaning of the word *diffidence* (line 9)?
   A. diversity
   B. care
   C. rigor
   D. arrogance
   E. timidity

4. The purpose of irony as used in lines 30-31 is to
   A. show the care that must be put into an effective lie.
   B. suggest that lies are more advantageous and commonplace than truth.
   C. castigate people who lie injudiciously.
   D. express contempt for people who are too idealistic to lie.
   E. discuss the differences between public and private lies.

5. What is the purpose of the lie told in paragraph 4?
   A. to hide the ladies' fervent desire to see their friends
   B. to fulfill an unspoken social obligation
   C. to make their sixteen hosts feel better about themselves
   D. to demonstrate the "intelligence and honor" in their hearts
   E. to cover up a breach of etiquette

6. What might be the best alternative title for this passage?
   A. The Case for Brutal Truth
   B. The Immorality of Deceit
   C. Lying – Evil or Euphemism?
   D. Honesty is the Best Policy
   E. Truth and Lies in Other Countries

7. The overall tone of this passage is
   A. pedantic and scholarly.
   B. authoritative and impartial.
   C. sardonic and scornful.
   D. learned and informative.
   E. facetious and satiric.

8. What is the best way to paraphrase the sentence below (line 35)?

   "The principle of truth may itself be carried into an absurdity."

   A. Being honest is ridiculous.
   B. Too much candor makes one ludicrous.
   C. People who follow principles are often persecuted with scorn.
   D. Carrying one's emotions around openly can lead to ridicule.
   E. Lying is a normal, everyday practice.

9. According to paragraph 3, what has come to be a "shame to our civilization"?
   A. the ignorance of the general population
   B. the fact that people do not habitually tell the truth anymore
   C. the deceptive attitudes that characterize many people
   D. the fact that there are people who think they are always honest
   E. the idea that a truth-teller would be impossible to live with

10. This passage would most likely be found in
    A. a journal of American history.
    B. a doctoral dissertation.
    C. the opinion/editorial section of a newspaper.
    D. a religious speech.
    E. a handbook of literary criticism.

REVIEW

Lessons 8 – 14

EXERCISE I – Sentence Completion

Choose the best pair of words to complete the sentence. Most choices will fit grammatically and will even make sense logically, but you must choose the pair that best fits the idea of the sentence.

Note that these words are not taken directly from lessons in this book. This exercise is intended to replicate the sentence completion portion of the SAT.

1. Scientists quickly discovered that they could obtain the ___________ results only if they combined the ___________ chemicals at one specific rate.
   A. desired, disparate
   B. explosive, thirteen
   C. proper, collected
   D. scholarly, tiny
   E. inconclusive, ordinary

2. Young people today increasingly purchase food based on ___________ and ___________ rather than excellence.
   A. quality, desirability
   B. reputation, taste
   C. price, speed
   D. nutrition, endorsements
   E. recommendations, location

3. ___________ to the pleadings of his victims, the movie ___________ continued to terrorize the town.
   A. Indifferent, villain
   B. Sensitive, character
   C. Responding, creature
   D. Answering, director
   E. Oblivious, star

4. To ___________ the rebellion, the British troops tried to starve the American colonists into ___________.
   A. quell, submission
   B. dispel, obeying
   C. relinquish, elimination
   D. facilitate, martyrdom
   E. end, weakness

5. Obtaining the proper ____________ from local officials before beginning construction was __________ to the completion of the project.
   A. credentials, inimical
   B. tools, essential
   C. clearance, integral
   D. paperwork, unnecessary
   E. permits, close

6. The Army commander needed to ____________ the remaining troops so they could best defend the entire ___________ of the fort against an attack from any direction.
   A. martial, area
   B. marshal, circumference
   C. gather, population
   D. force, wealth
   E. order, insides

7. Even though the orchestra reached the stormiest portion of the symphony, it seemed as though each __________ note possessed its own __________ quality.
   A. individual, tenuous
   B. vibrant, distinct
   C. unobtrusive, harmonious
   D. mellifluous, jarring
   E. concrete, placid

8. Automobiles, once considered the __________ of a[n] __________ upper class, were made accessible to common people after Henry Ford introduced the Model T.
   A. idea, mobile
   B. province, elitist
   C. symbol, impoverished
   D. material, energetic
   E. status, huge

EXERCISE II – Crossword Puzzle

Use the clues to complete the crossword puzzle. The answers consist of vocabulary words from lessons 8 through 14.

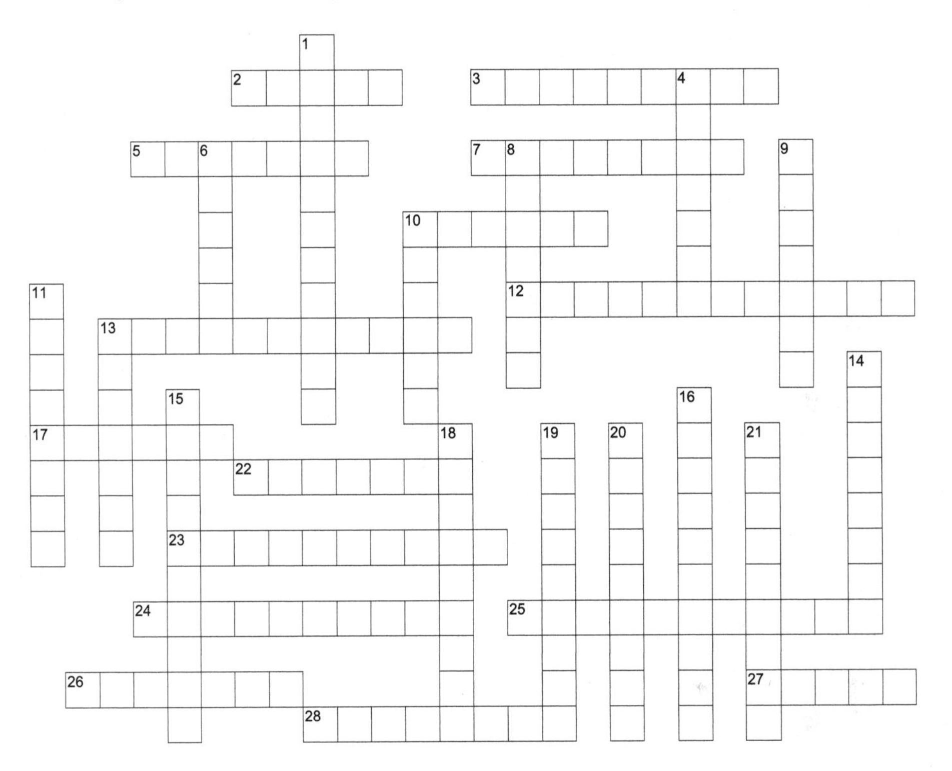

Across
2. to summon
3. relevant
5. friendly
7. sorrowful
10. likeness
12. stubborn
13. fight
17. strong point
22. to explain
23. insatiable
24. to bypass
25. unclear
26. difficult
27. to lessen
28. lecture

Down
1. to cooperate
4. to imitate
6. inconstant
8. threatening
9. propriety
10. to encourage
11. bitterness
13. strict
14. regretful
15. deadly
16. overjoyed
18. admiration
19. to spur into action
20. to deplore
21. a fraud

Lesson Fifteen

1. **noxious** (nok´ shəs) *adj.* harmful to the health
   We opened a window to remove the *noxious* fumes of the paint thinner.
   syn: injurious *ant: harmless*

2. **connive** (kə nīv´) *v.* to cooperate secretly in wrongdoing
   The corrupt judge *connived* with crooked politicians in order to make himself rich.
   syn: conspire

3. **chutzpah** (hoot´ spə) *n.* nerve; audacity
   I cannot believe Michael had the *chutzpah* to claim that no one could sing that song as well as he could.
   syn: brazenness; effrontery *ant: timidity*

4. **liege** (lēj) *n.* a lord, master, or sovereign
   While the servants pledged their loyalty to the *liege*, they did not always like or respect him.
   syn: king *ant: commoner; servant*

5. **odium** (ō´ dē əm) *n.* hatred
   The rebels had only *odium* for the ruling party.
   syn: abhorrence *ant: love; adoration*

6. **crass** (kras) *adj.* coarse; tasteless
   Ben made a *crass* comment about the length of the waitress's skirt.
   syn: crude *ant: refined*

7. **hypercritical** (hī pər krit´ i kəl) *adj.* overcritical; too severe in judgment
   In his inspection of the barracks, the sergeant was so *hypercritical* that no one passed.
   syn: faultfinding *ant: lax*

8. **fallacy** (fal´ ə sē) *n.* a mistaken notion; a misconception
   My grandmother still clings to the *fallacy* that the world is flat.
   ant: truth

9. **complacent** (kəm plā´ sənt) *adj.* self-satisfied; smug
   The former heavyweight champion became *complacent* after easily defeating several amateur boxers.
   syn: assured; confident *ant: humble*

10. **befuddle** (bi fud´ l) *v.* to confuse; to perplex
Street maps always *befuddle* me, so my girlfriend navigates when we take road trips.
syn: bewilder; fluster *ant: clarify; elucidate*

11. **pandemonium** (pan də mō´ nē əm) *n.* a wild disorder, noise, or confusion
Feeding time at the zoo could be *pandemonium* if not done slowly and carefully.
syn: chaos; tumult; din *ant: order; calm*

12. **parsimonious** (pär sə mō´ nē əs) *adj.* excessively thrifty; stingy
Ebenezer Scrooge was a *parsimonious* old man.
syn: cheap; frugal *ant: extravagant*

13. **verbose** (vər bōs´) *adj.* using more words than are needed; wordy
Some find Charles Dickens so *verbose* that they swear he must have been paid by the word.
syn: prolix *ant:* terse; concise; succinct

14. **laudable** (lô´ də bəl) *adj.* worthy of praise; commendable
The city has made *laudable* efforts to reduce crime by introducing after-school programs.
syn: admirable *ant: execrable*

15. **indiscreet** (in di skrēt´) *adj.* not wise or judicious; imprudent, as in speech or action
Ron was fired shortly after his *indiscreet* actions at the office party.
syn: flagrant *ant: prudent*

EXERCISE I—Words in Context

From the list below, supply the words needed to complete the paragraph. Some words will not be used.

odium	**laudable**	**connived**	**verbose**	**befuddle**
fallacy	**noxious**	**chutzpah**	**crass**	**pandemonium**

A. If the company representative had arrived another minute later, the crowd would have erupted into __________. Since discovering the hidden toxic dump behind a residential neighborhood, most of the residents felt a great deal of __________ for Kraytron officials. The whole mess began just two weeks before, when children became ill from __________ vapors in the forest next to their development. Two days, one evacuation, and one hazardous material response team later, town officials declared the site to be an illegal dump for hazardous waste. Though a thorough investigation would take months, if not years, most of the town's residents immediately concluded that Kraytron officials must have __________ with a few greedy locals in an effort to avoid the cost of waste disposal.

When the booing and taunting finally stopped, the __________ Greg Haxton began his ninety-minute speech. Unknown to the public, Haxton had been Kraytron's unofficial crowd control specialist for over ten years.

"Your concern for your environment is indeed __________," said Greg. "It's good to see a community that can pull together in a predicament." Greg continued with his positive observations for five minutes before coming to the reason for his speech. "I know that many of you are assuming that Kraytron created the dump because the factory is only two miles from the site. This rumor is a complete __________; the officials have already dated the site as being at least twenty years old—ten years before Kraytron even constructed the local facility. The dump can be attributed to the __________ decisions of the former Mattingdon Aluminum Mill officials; they ran the mill here for forty years before going bankrupt two decades ago. To those of you who are Kraytron employees, you must understand that Kraytron would never have the __________ to commit such a heinous crime against its own family."

From the list below, supply the words needed to complete the paragraph. Some words will not be used.

befuddle	**liege**	**parsimonious**
chutzpah	**complacent**	**hypercritical**

B. "Come on, Jennifer, just buy a bag of charcoal! What are you going to save? Maybe a dime? I have never met a teenager as __________ as you."

Silently mocking Julie, Jennifer grabbed the first bag of charcoal on the shelf. She knew that they were late for the cookout, but Julie's __________ attitude sometimes annoyed her. To Jennifer, it seemed as though Julie was always finding fault. They checked out at the register and walked to the car.

"I'm sorry if this __________ you," remarked Jennifer, "but as it stands, we're broke, which means that we need to watch our spending. You've blown way too much money lately."

Julie didn't reply immediately; she just sat in the patchwork seat of the primer-colored subcompact with a[n] __________ look on her face. As Jennifer turned the key, she heard Julie mumble a facetious "Yes, my __________."

EXERCISE II—Sentence Completion

Complete the sentence in a way that shows you understand the meaning of the italicized vocabulary word.

1. *Pandemonium* ensued at the stadium when…

2. Though she was a millionaire, the *parsimonious* woman still…

3. Your *verbose* lecture is causing the audience to…

4. The *liege* had only minutes to live, for the assassins were…

5. While working around *noxious* paint fumes, be sure to…

6. The emergency planning committee has made a *laudable* effort to protect the city from…

7. Leonard's *crass* demeanor sometimes caused Elmira to…

8. The *complacent* security guard had no idea that…

9. Though the apartment was immaculate, Lee's *hypercritical* mother still found…

10. The crooked commissioner *connived* with the mobster to…

11. Tawnya had the *chutzpah* to tell the speaker that…

12. Your *odium* for authority is only going to…

13. The *indiscreet* agent revealed his identity during…

14. Many people are guilty of believing the *fallacy* that…

15. Complicated math problems always *befuddled* Gene, which is why he…

EXERCISE III—Roots, Prefixes, and Suffixes

Study the entries and answer the questions that follow.

The roots *loqu* and *locut* mean "speak, talk."
The roots *pend* and *pens* mean "hang."
The root *gest* means "carry" or "bring."
The suffix *cy* means "the state or position of."
The prefix *e* means "out."

A. Using literal translations as guidance, define the following words without using a dictionary:

1. elocution
2. loquacious
3. eloquent
4. pendant
5. dependency
6. gestation

B. The crowd eagerly awaited the ____________________ outcome of the horse race while the judges analyzed the photo finish.

C. A *gesture* is a motion of the body that is used to express or emphasize ideas or emotions. Gesture comes from the root *gest*, but how is the word related to this root?

D. List as many words as you can think of that contain the roots *loqu, locut,* and *gest.*

EXERCISE IV—Inference

Complete the sentences by inferring information about the italicized word from its context.

A. If I am *hypercritical* while reviewing your work, and then you find a mistake in my work, you might tell me…

B. When the assembly instructions for a new appliance *befuddle* you, it is a good idea to…

C. When your boss reads your *indiscreet* remarks about the company in tomorrow's paper, she will probably…

EXERCISE V—Writing

Here is a writing prompt similar to the one you will find on the writing portion of the SAT.

Plan and write an essay based on the following statement:

> Genius is a strange, intangible force. It is an undefinable, peculiar something that possesses a certain class of extraordinary human beings and gives vent to itself in a manner that impresses and confounds mortals.
>
> – Elwood S. Brown, The Promoter; His Genius
> From a collection under the title
> *Clever Business Sketches*, 1909

Assignment: In an essay, discuss the merit of Brown's appraisal of genius. Use evidence from your reading, your studies, your observations, and your experience to support your opinion.

Thesis: Write a *one-sentence* response to the above assignment. Make certain this single sentence offers a clear statement of your position.
Example: Elwood Brown labels geniuses as impressive and confounding, but his failure to describe an actual genius leaves too many open questions to make his definition valid.

Organizational Plan: If your thesis is the point on which you want to end, where does your essay need to begin? List the points of development that are inevitable in leading your reader from your beginning point to your end point. This list is your outline.

Draft: Use your thesis as both your beginning and your end. Following your outline, write a good first draft of your essay. Remember to support all your points with examples, facts, references to reading, etc.

Review and Revise: Exchange essays with a classmate. Using the scoring guide for Sentence Formation and Variety on page 208, score your partner's essay (while he or she scores yours). Focus on the sentence structure and use of language conventions. If necessary, rewrite your essay to improve the sentence structure and the use of language.

Improving Paragraphs

Read the following passage and then answer the multiple-choice questions that follow. Note that the questions will require you to make decisions regarding the revision of the reading selection.

(1) The physical condition and various impairments of maturation notwithstanding, the mental age of some people seems to advance quickly to the state of "old age." (2) Some people seem to age more quickly than others do.

(3) There are those who simply sit down, grow old, and act old. (4) Let us call them the Agers. (5) This "aging" state frequently comes on right after retirement, but is not limited to any chronological age, because some people retire as early as 45.

(6) Agers seem to congregate with one another as though they have nowhere else to turn. (7) Being alone doesn't seem to be favored by Agers, because they are seldom seen that way.

(8) Conversely, there are people who are in age-denial; but by their actions, they display a young frame of mind by acting young. (9) Let us call them Everteens. (10) Certainly, people in their seventies or eighties might have fallen victim to any number of age-related afflictions such as arthritis, high blood pressure, hearing loss and poor eyesight. (11) Everteens don't seem to complain about their infirmities, aren't bothered by being alone, and take life as it comes. (12) They are often seen walking alone behind a shopping cart, having coffee, and sitting in a library or on a park bench reading the newspaper.

(13) How is this phenomenon of diverse states explained. (14) One interpretation is that if a baby boy is born more than three minutes late, he is automatically born old. (15) If a baby girl is born more than seven days late, she is born old. (16) There appears to be some correlation between these date determinations and the sell-by dates on perishable food items. (17) It would be advisable if doctors who deliver babies were made aware of this theory so they would let no baby be born after its time.

1. Which of the following revisions would improve the first paragraph?
   A. Reverse the order of sentences 1 and 2.
   B. Delete sentence 2.
   C. Remove the quotation marks.
   D. Change the initial *seems* to *seem*.
   E. Rewrite sentence 6.

2. Which of the following revisions would better develop continuity after the first paragraph?
   A. Begin paragraph 2 with sentence 4.
   B. Reverse the second and third paragraphs.
   C. Exchange sentences 6 and 7 in paragraph 3.
   D. Write out the figure 45.
   E. Combine paragraphs 2 and 3.

3. If you had to delete an unnecessary sentence in paragraph 4, which one would you choose?
   A. Sentence 8
   B. Sentence 9
   C. Sentence 10
   D. Sentence 11
   E. Sentence 12

4. Which choice describes the first error in paragraph 5?
   A. The word *three* should be written as the number 3.
   B. There is no question mark after the first sentence.
   C. The words *sell-by* do not need a hyphen.
   D. The word *doctor* should be capitalized.
   E. There is no error in the last paragraph.

5. In the final paragraph, which sentence could be removed without changing the intent of the piece?
   A. Sentence 13
   B. Sentence 14
   C. Sentence 15
   D. Sentence 16
   E. Sentence 17

Lesson Sixteen

1. **pique** (pēk) *v.* to cause resentment; to provoke
   The old gentleman was *piqued* because he was not given a seat at the head table.
   syn: irritate *ant: assuage*

2. **linguistics** (ling gwis´ tiks) *n.* the scientific study of the structure, sounds, and meaning of language
   The professor of *linguistics* explained how English evolved from a number of other languages.

3. **plebeian** (pli bē´ ən) *n.* a commoner; one from the lower class
   adj. common or vulgar
   (n.) Seniors treated the freshmen as though they were *plebeians*.
   (a.) The baroness refused to do the *plebian* chores of cooking and cleaning.
   (n.) *syn: peon; peasant* *ant: liege*
   (a.) *syn: base; lowly* *ant: refined; aristocratic*

4. **precocious** (pri kō´ shəs) *adj.* showing early development, especially mental
   Anthony was such a *precocious* three-year-old that he could already play the violin well.
   syn: advanced

5. **predatory** (pred´ ə tôr ē) *adj.* inclined to prey on others
   The buzzard is a scavenger, but the hawk is a *predatory* animal.
   syn: pillaging; despoiling *ant: nurturing*

6. **prowess** (prow´ is) *n.* superior skill or ability
   Ty's physical *prowess* was matched by his superior mental ability.
   syn: strength; dominance; power *ant: weakness*

7. **pugnacious** (pug nā´ shəs) *adj.* eager and ready to fight; quarrelsome
   Because he was so *pugnacious*, he had few friends.
   syn: combative; belligerent *ant: placid; pacific*

8. **purloin** (pər loin´) *v.* to steal
   They had not planned to *purloin* the jewels, but the temptation was too great.
   syn: burglarize

9. **pusillanimous** (pyōō sə lan´ ə məs) *adj.* cowardly; fearful
   The Wizard of Oz granted the *pusillanimous* lion his wish to have courage.
   syn: fainthearted; timid *ant: brave; bold*

10. **quell** (kwel) *v.* to put an end to; to allay or quiet
The police were called in to *quell* the riot.
syn: calm *ant: foment; incite*

11. **quixotic** (kwik sot´ ik) *adj.* very idealistic; impractical; caught up in romantic notions
As a young man, he had the *quixotic* notion that he could single-handedly end poverty in the country.
ant: realistic; practical

12. **rabble** (rab´ əl) *n.* a disorderly crowd, a mob
The guards had to protect the president from the *rabble* in the streets.
syn: riffraff

13. **rabid** (rab´ id) *adj.* raging; fanatical
After working out, Chrissy had a *rabid* thirst and drank two gallons of water.
syn: uncontrollable; fervid *ant: placid*

14. **raconteur** (rak on tyûr´) *n.* a person skilled at telling stories
An exceptional *raconteur*, Lorna held the whole audience spellbound with her stories.

15. **vindictive** (vin dik´ tiv) *adj.* seeking revenge; bearing a grudge
Out of some *vindictive* urge, Steve slashed his ex-girlfriend's tires.
syn: vengeful *ant: forgiving*

EXERCISE I—Words in Context

From the list below, supply the words needed to complete the paragraph. Some words will not be used.

quell	**linguistics**	**vindictive**	**rabble**
prowess	**purloin**	**pugnacious**	

A. "Your __________ on the field does not excuse your __________ behavior at school. This is the second time that you've been in trouble for fighting," said the principal. She hated this situation; she knew what to do, but in the way the school perceived her, it would be a lose-lose decision. Punishing Isaac before the district championship game would surely draw a[n] __________ of angry students and parents to her office. Being lenient with Isaac would fuel the already __________ attitudes of second-offenders throughout the school. The turbulent aftermath of either decision would be difficult to __________.

From the list below, supply the words needed to complete the paragraph. Some words will not be used.

plebeian pique raconteur quell linguistics precocious

B. Everyone had high hopes for the __________ youngster. At the age of six, Mariah seemed to have such a command of __________ that a simple conversation with her could __________ even the brightest of her classmates; consequently, they felt more as though they were speaking to an adult than a kindergartner. She also loved to exercise her fine speaking abilities. Never at a loss for words, the young __________ would come home from school every night and vividly describe the events of her day to her parents.

From the list below, supply the words needed to complete the paragraph. Some words will not be used.

plebeian quixotic linguistics pusillanimous
predatory rabid purloin

C. Owing in part to his __________ interest in the heroic tales of Arthur's knights and high adventures set in the Middle Ages, Delmar had a rather __________ perspective of the world. He never simply "went to work" or "picked up a burger at the drive-through"; instead, Delmar lived in a fantasy world in which each day he had to uphold his chivalric duty while challenging a myriad of perilous obstacles. The pigeons on the roof of his apartment were not pigeons—they were great __________, winged beasts, perpetually waiting to swoop down and __________ Delmar's poppyseed bagel as he walked to his chariot—a rusty Ford Granada that had recently passed the two-hundred-thousand-mile mark. After a short ride to the Hall of Lords (the metro station), Delmar would spend the day protecting the ignorant __________ from microscopic legions of evil warriors, mainly by spraying all surfaces with disinfectant before wiping them down with a rag. Evil dirt warriors were not Delmar's greatest problem; sometimes he had to confront the mystical rat-beasts that lived in the basement storage area. Indeed, the basement was no place for __________ folk—only knights as brave as Sir Delmar.

EXERCISE II—Sentence Completion

Complete the sentence in a way that shows you understand the meaning of the italicized vocabulary word.

1. Carnivorous *predatory* animals will eat meat before they will eat...

2. The filthy tavern was full of *pugnacious* characters looking for...

3. Let's see if your *prowess* during practice extends to the...

4. The *rabble* outside the governor's mansion chanted about the new policy on...

5. The tear gas easily *quelled* the protestors at...

6. The audience was engrossed with the old *raconteur's* accounts of...

7. Everyone knew that Colt was too *pusillanimous* to ever become a professional...

8. The *quixotic* Dexter thought that he alone could someday...

9. The new *linguistics* teacher claimed that writing was just as important as...

10. After three days of surviving in the wilderness, the co-pilot's *rabid* hunger drove her to...

11. The dressmaker *piqued* Linda by pointing out that she...

12. Still *vindictive* about losing the promotion to a younger associate, Elvira made life...

13. After he *purloined* the company secrets, Sol went to the competition and...

14. The *precocious* preschooler was already good at...

15. The greedy Duke never responded to the *plebeian* requests for...

EXERCISE III—Roots, Prefixes, and Suffixes

Study the entries and answer the questions that follow.

The root *man* means "hand."
The suffix *escent* means "becoming."
The roots *nat* and *nas* mean "born."
The prefix *in* means "in."
The prefix *re* means "again."

A. *Using literal translations as guidance, define the following words without using a dictionary:*

1. manacles
2. innate
3. nativity
4. nascent
5. renascence
6. manicure

B. Literally, *manual labor* is labor ________________.
The word "manufacture" contains two roots: __________ and __________.
It literally means ________________________.
Manipulation literally refers to ________________________________,
and the word *manuscript* literally means ________________________.

C. A *mandate* is an order or a command. How do you think this word got its meaning?

D. List all the words you can think of that have the suffix *escent*.

E. List all the words that you can think of that contain the roots *nat* or *nas*.

EXERCISE IV—Inference

Complete the sentences by inferring information about the italicized word from its context.

A. Gwendolyn and the Duke of Trombonia loved each other, but since Gwendolyn was a *plebeian*, they…

B. Geoff is very *pugnacious*, so if someone accidentally spills a beverage on him, he will probably…

C. If the police are sent to *quell* a riot, they might…

EXERCISE V—Critical Reading

Below is a reading passage followed by several multiple-choice questions similar to the ones you will encounter on the SAT. Carefully read the passage and choose the best answer to each of the questions.

The author of this passage is commenting on the creation of empires.

1 A system of trade transpires when a nation's demand for goods obliges it to seek the goods from other nations. England needed goods that it could not produce because of an improper climate or a lack of necessary resources; consequently, it sent explorers to find the goods in foreign lands. The exploration found not only the required goods, but new, previously unknown lands and peoples with whom England could establish new commerce. The discovery of the new lands was an impetus for travel and colonization, which in turn resulted in new technology and economic advancement of the mother country.

2 Even in its early stages, a functional system of international trade required considerable travel and enormous logistical effort. To ensure the success of established trade routes, merchants had to maintain a presence in other nations, especially those that were undeveloped and thus potential trade partners for other nations. These agents, or representatives, would establish trading posts in which they could acquire the native goods and transfer them to the traders or merchants. As trade increased, more people were required to support acquisition efforts. In response to growing demand, England established colonies that were capable of conducting the necessary business while protecting goods, shipments, and relations with the host nations; however, relations were not always ideal for the natives. Many of the merchant colonists sought advancement in social status, and they favored the idea that despite having a low social status at home, they were far superior to the often-primitive natives. On the grounds of their perceived superiority, colonists acquired goods, land, and labor at little cost. Mother countries sought to "civilize" the natives, which, to the colonists, meant compelling the natives to emulate the language, culture, and religion of the mother country.

3 Expansion of trade forced leaps in technology, beginning with advancements in transportation. The growing number of colonists and merchants required a means of transporting themselves and their goods. Larger and faster ships emerged, allowing more efficient international commerce. Traders could transfer more goods, make more frequent trips, and communicate more quickly with their counterparts abroad. The invention of the telegraph accelerated commerce even more, because merchants could instantly exchange knowledge about demand, prices, or shipping details across great distances. Medical advancements also increased commerce; the discovery of quinine helped traders to overcome the deadly malaria that was rampant throughout certain colonies. By diminishing the threat of disease, traders and colonists could remain in foreign lands for extended periods while pushing inland to expand trade opportunities.

4 After establishing an efficient system of international trade, the mother country was able to soar to economic superiority and relieve its own abundance of goods, particularly those made using the raw materials imported from colonies. The mother country manufactured products from the goods and exported them back to

the colonized country—a process that was patently unfair to the colonized country but especially profitable for the mother country, which consequently increased in wealth. To protect these interests, the mother country maintained a military presence in the colonies while forcing the assimilation of the natives to its own cultural and political systems. Eventually, smaller countries in the trade network would be forced to limit trade to only the mother country, thus making them economically dependent. They became small components of what is defined as an empire.

1. The primary purpose of this passage is to
   A. explain why trade is good.
   B. suggest how trade was a dominant force in the creation of empires.
   C. explain the forces present in the creation of empires.
   D. suggest how the discovery of new lands contributes to the creation of empires.
   E. show how an empire increases trade.

2. The overall tone of this passage is
   A. entertaining.
   B. thoughtful.
   C. simplistic.
   D. scholarly.
   E. anecdotal.

3. According to paragraph two, initial colonization resulted from the need to
   A. have trade representatives in the distant nations.
   B. help people advance in social status.
   C. allow people to be superior to the natives.
   D. find places to send missionaries.
   E. civilize the natives.

4. As used in paragraph one, *mother* means
   A. one who gives birth.
   B. a female parent.
   C. a woman of authority.
   D. the source or origin of something.
   E. a woman of authority.

5. Which of the following best paraphrases the sentence, "Mother countries sought to 'civilize' the natives, which, to the colonists, meant compelling the natives to emulate the language, culture, and religion of the mother country" (paragraph 2)?
   A. The British were the only civilized people.
   B. Colonists thought they were the only civilized people.
   C. All native cultures were uncivilized.
   D. Colonists were superior to all people.
   E. The British wanted to make all people like themselves.

6. Which of the following is an example of how technology did *not* grow because of trade?
   A. the development of larger ships
   B. the development of faster ships
   C. the invention of the telegraph
   D. the discovery of quinine
   E. the development of mass production

7. As used in paragraph three, *quinine* most likely means a type of
   A. beverage.
   B. precious metal.
   C. medicine.
   D. transportation.
   E. weapon.

8. According to paragraph four, which is not a reason why trade is beneficial?
   A. disposal of extra goods
   B. attainment of wanted goods
   C. ability to manufacture products
   D. higher revenue for the mother country
   E. restricted trade for smaller countries

9. Which choice would be the best title for this passage?
   A. Trade as a Dominant Force in Creating Empires
   B. Trade and the Results
   C. How Empires are Created
   D. Trade, Travel, and Technology
   E. Empires and Their Economies

10. This passage would most likely be found in
    A. an encyclopedia of economics.
    B. a book of empires.
    C. a doctoral dissertation.
    D. a world history book.
    E. an American history book.

Lesson Seventeen

1. **circumspect** (sûr´ kəm spekt) *adj.* careful; heedful; attentive to all points
   Although I tried to be *circumspect* when packing for camp, I never guessed that I should have packed an extra clock.
   syn: judicious; prudent *ant: rash; foolhardy*

2. **zephyr** (zef´ ər) *n.* a gentle breeze (sometimes specifically the West Wind)
   A sweet-smelling *zephyr* ruffled the laundry on the line.
   ant: gale

3. **renegade** (ren´ i gād) *n.* one who deserts one side in favor of another; traitor; outlaw
   The members of the old party called him a *renegade*; the members of his new party called him a patriot.
   syn: turncoat; defector *ant: loyalist*

4. **retribution** (ret rə byōō´ shən) *n.* something justly deserved, especially a punishment
   The boys had to spend the weekend picking up litter in *retribution* for having spray-painted graffiti on the bus.
   syn: reprisal *ant: reward*

5. **hurtle** (hûr´ tl) *v.* to move or to fling swiftly and with great force
   The big fullback *hurtled* his way through the defensive line and scored the winning touchdown.
   syn: hurl

6. **scourge** (skûrj) *n.* a person or thing that causes great trouble or misfortune
   Cancer remains one of the worst *scourges* of mankind.
   syn: torment; bane; curse *ant: boon; blessing*

7. **caustic** (kô´ stik) *adj.* biting; stingingly sharp or sarcastic
   Because of his *caustic* comments, his wife finally left him.
   syn: acidic; harsh *ant: mild; pleasant*

8. **taciturn** (tas´ i tûrn) *adj.* not fond of talking; usually silent
   We were amazed when the *taciturn* young man signed up for public speaking.
   syn: reticent; reserved *ant: garrulous; loquacious; talkative*

9. **agnostic** (ag nos´ tik) *n.* one who believes that the existence of God can neither be proved nor disproved
Although he did not officially believe in God, the *agnostic* sometimes prayed "just in case."
syn: skeptic *ant: believer*

10. **terse** (tûrs) *adj.* brief and to the point
Julia didn't give me any details about her break-up, just a *terse*,"it's over."
syn: abbreviated; curt *ant: verbose; rambling*

11. **uncanny** (un kan´ ē) *adj.* weird; strange; so keen or acute as to seem bizarre
Tess had an *uncanny* memory for details; she knew exactly what she had worn on any given day in the past eleven years.
syn: eerie

12. **exodus** (ek´ sə dəs) *n.* a mass departure or emigration
The many defeated tribes made a speedy *exodus* from the war-torn valley.
ant: return

13. **penitent** (pen´ i tənt) *adj.* remorseful; sorry for having done wrong
Seeing the boy's *penitent* expression, the judge was easier on him than he might otherwise have been.
syn: apologetic *ant: unrepentant*

14. **vindicate** (vin´ di kāt) *v.* to clear of suspicion or accusations
Darren sued for libel in order to *vindicate* his reputation.
syn: exonerate; acquit *ant: besmirch; implicate*

15. **raillery** (rā´ lə rē) *n.* good-humored ridicule or teasing
James much prefers Carson's *raillery* to the cynical slurs of other comedians.
syn: banter

EXERCISE I—Words in Context

From the list below, supply the words needed to complete the paragraph. Some words will not be used.

penitent	**hurtle**	**agnostic**	**scourge**
circumspect	**retribution**	**zephyr**	**exodus**

A. Sergeant Neil Newman, one of six mine removal experts in Southeast Asia, makes sure that he is __________ about every aspect of his job.

"One little missed detail can result in tragedy becoming __________ for your hastiness. One minute you're on your knees, probing the earth and enjoying a cool __________ after hours of 95-degree weather, and the next minute, a blast __________ you—or a part of you—through the air because you overlooked a hair-thin tripwire. By that time, it's too late to be __________ about your error—you're lucky if you're still alive to think about it."

The uncharted minefields that Neil faces have been a[n] __________ on war-torn nations for decades, and experts estimate that it will take people like Neil hundreds of years to find and neutralize the millions of underground threats.

From the list below, supply the words needed to complete the paragraph. Some words will not be used.

raillery	**vindicate**	**terse**	**taciturn**
hurtle	**uncanny**	**exodus**	**renegade**

B. The __________ Haley silently stared at her console despite the elated atmosphere of the command center. While everyone celebrated the latest victory of the rebel forces, Haley received a message that would soon turn the celebration into panic. Two __________ had revealed the secret location of the command center, and as soon as she gave the word, the entire facility would have to prepare for a[n] __________ to a new location before the Nationalist forces arrived. The Nationalists had a[n] __________ ability to turn the rebels against each other; this would be the third time in three months that the rebels were forced to relocate their base of operations. Haley took a breath, swiveled around in her chair, and prepared to deliver a[n] __________ briefing that would squelch the group's cheerful air. To make matters worse, one of the traitors turned out to be Haley's cousin, a lieutenant whom Haley recently helped __________ from espionage charges.

From the list below, supply the words needed to complete the paragraph. Some words will not be used.

terse raillery caustic agnostic scourge

C. Paige and Mia have been friends for more than twenty years, despite the fact that Paige is devoutly religious and Mia is a[n] __________. They often have heated discussions about religion, but their conversation inevitably turns into good-humored __________. Over the years, they learned to avoid making __________ comments during arguments, no matter how angry they might get.

EXERCISE II—Sentence Completion

Complete the sentence in a way that shows you understand the meaning of the italicized vocabulary word.

1. The workers were thankful for the *zephyr* as they labored through the…
2. The victims of the bombing demanded *retribution* for their…
3. The asteroid *hurtled* toward earth, giving the people only minutes to…
4. Sheila's *caustic* tongue made her supervisor think twice about…
5. Major Buchanan gave a *terse* briefing about the invading squadron of…
6. The eastern acrobatic trio had the *uncanny* ability to…
7. Urik's family finally *vindicated* him after he spent eight years in prison for…
8. Though his parents were quite religious, Thomas remained *agnostic* in…
9. The *renegade* mercenary quietly left his platoon in order to…
10. The *circumspect* bomb technician noticed that the suspect device was…
11. Good humored *raillery* did not please the new teacher, who in turn…
12. The maniacal dictator was a *scourge* on mankind until…
13. The *taciturn* Willow surprised everyone when she decided to become…
14. The penitent *fugitive* decided to stop running and…
15. As the last stone was removed from the cave entrance, an *exodus* of…

EXERCISE III—Roots, Prefixes, and Suffixes

Study the entries and answer the questions that follow.

The root *phil* means "love" or "loving."
The root *ocul* means "eye."
The root *mar* means "sea."
The prefix *sub* means "under."

A. *Using literal translations as guidance, define the following words without using a dictionary:*

1. philanthropy	4. ocular
2. philharmonic	5. oculist
3. maritime	6. submarine

B. The root *sophos* means wise, so a *philosopher* is one who ____________ ________________.

The root *moros* means "foolish" or "fool"; therefore, the literal meaning of "sophomore" is ____.

C. *Phile* is sometimes found at the end of a word. What do you suppose the following people love?
anglophiles:
francophiles:
bibliophiles:

D. List all the words you can think of that contain the roots *phil*, *ocul* or *mar*.

EXERCISE IV—Inference

Complete the sentences by inferring information about the italicized word from its context.

A. If Mr. Reckner cannot *vindicate* himself from the charges of grand larceny, he will probably…

B. Damian, who went to school despite the fact that he was sick with influenza, became the *scourge* of his class when…

C. The pianist didn't even need an electronic tuner; she had the *uncanny* ability to…

EXERCISE V—Writing

Here is a writing prompt similar to the one you will find on the writing portion of the SAT.

Plan and write an essay based on the following statement:

> In August of 1862, Horace Greeley, editor of the *New York Tribune*, wrote an editorial in which he criticized President Abraham Lincoln's administration as "lacking direction and resolve," and in which he demanded the emancipation of American slaves. A few days later, Abraham Lincoln sent a reply in which he said, "My paramount object in this struggle is to save the Union....If I could save the Union without freeing any slave, I would do it; and if I could save it by freeing all the slaves, I would do it; and if I could save it by freeing some and leaving others alone, I would also do that."

Assignment: Write an essay in which you explain Lincoln's response to Horace Greeley. Use evidence from your reading, your studies, your observations, and your experience to support and develop your points of explanation.

Thesis: Write a *one-sentence* response to the above assignment. Make certain this single sentence offers a clear statement of your position.
Example: According to President Abraham Lincoln, the purpose of the Civil War was to preserve the Union—not to end the evils of slavery.

Organizational Plan: If your thesis is the point on which you want to end, where does your essay need to begin? List the points of development that are inevitable in leading your reader from your beginning point to your end point. This list is your outline.

Draft: Use your thesis as both your beginning and your end. Following your outline, write a good first draft of your essay. Remember to support all your points with examples, facts, references to reading, etc.

Review and Revise: Exchange essays with a classmate. Using the scoring guide for Word Choice on page 209, score your partner's essay (while he or she scores yours). Focus on word choice and the use of language conventions. If necessary, rewrite your essay to improve the word choice and use of language.

Identifying Sentence Errors

Identify the errors in the following sentences. If the sentence contains no error, select answer E.

1. When the warden agreed to us (A) that the prisoner should be released (B), we were pleased to accept (C) the invitation to the parole hearing. (D) No error. (E)

2. The new park project (A) for underprivileged (B) children was began (C) in the spring but will not be completed (D) until late November. No error. (E)

3. Last year we had (A) an especially severe winter and despite our efforts (B) to remove the snow, it had lain (C) on the barn roof all season. (D) No error. (E)

4. When all the votes are in (A) and are counted (B), it alone (C) will decide the next governor (D) of this fine state. No error. (E)

5. The speaker at the horse-breeders' convention would have been (A) better if she took the time (B) to prepare (C) for the subjects of interest to the audience. (D) No error. (E)

Improving Sentences

The underlined portion of each sentence below contains some flaw. Select the answer that best corrects the flaw.

6. The aging movie star was particular about her appearance and was as particularly engaging as ever when she looked her best.
   A. was as particular as engaging as ever
   B. was as engaging particularly as ever
   C. was as ever particularly engaging
   D. was as engaging as ever
   E. was particularly engaging

7. We were bouncing a basketball in the driveway and a neighbor came over and told us we were making too much noise.
   A. When we were bouncing a basketball in the driveway, a neighbor came over to tell us we were making too much noise.
   B. A neighbor came over to tell us we were making too much noise and we were bouncing a basketball in the driveway.
   C. We were bouncing a basketball when a neighbor in the driveway came over to tell us we were making too much noise.
   D. Bouncing a basketball, a neighbor came over and told us we were making too much noise in the driveway.
   E. When a neighbor came over and told us to bounce a basketball in the driveway, we were making too much noise.

8. Hoping for the support of his constituents was the incumbent candidate who ran against a strong opponent for the position of state senator.
   A. One incumbent state senator candidate ran against a strong opponent and hoped for his constituents' support.
   B. Hoping his constituents would support him, the incumbent candidate for state senator faced a strong opponent.
   C. Running against a strong opponent was an incumbent state senator candidate who hoped for the constituent support.
   D. Hoping to be state senator the incumbent candidate ran against a strong opponent and was hoping for the support of his constituents.
   E. The incumbent candidate was hoping for the support of his constituents when running against a strong opponent for state senator.

9. Alfred was able to secure a government job after he graduated from college which lasted for almost twenty years.
   A. Alfred lasted almost twenty years after he was able to secure a government job after he graduated from college.
   B. After he graduated from college which lasted for almost twenty years, Alfred was able to secure a government job.
   C. Alfred was able to graduate from college to secure a government job which lasted for almost twenty years.
   D. After graduating from college, Alfred was able to secure a government job that lasted for almost twenty years.
   E. For almost twenty years, Alfred was able to secure a government job after he graduated from college.

10. When children play in the street without any shoes and their mothers know about it and the neighbors don't tell them to stop.
    A. Children don't tell their neighbors to stop when they play in the street without shoes and their mothers know about it.
    B. When the children play without any shoes in the street, and their mothers know about it, the neighbors won't stop them from playing.
    C. When neighbors don't tell them to stop, children play in the street without any shoes and their mothers know about it.
    D. Without shoes, children play in the street and their mothers know about it and the neighbors don't tell them to stop.
    E. Their mothers know about it and children play in the street without shoes and the neighbors don't tell them to stop.

Lesson Eighteen

1. **impregnable** (im preg´ nə bəl) *adj.* not able to be conquered; impenetrable
   The Greek warriors were unable to conquer the *impregnable* Trojan fortress.
   syn: unbeatable *ant: vulnerable*

2. **xenophobia** (ze nə fō´ bē ə) *n.* an intense dislike or fear of strangers or foreigners
   Tim's *xenophobia* gave him an unwarranted hatred for immigrants coming to America.

3. **inherent** (in hir´ ənt) *adj.* essential
   Exhaust and air-pollution are *inherent* features and drawbacks of the automobile.
   syn: intrinsic *ant: extrinsic; extraneous*

4. **irreverent** (i rev´ rənt) *adj.* disrespectful
   John's *irreverent* attitude toward his pastor embarrassed and angered his mother.
   syn: insubordinate *ant: worshipful*

5. **subjugate** (sub´ ji gāt) *v.* to dominate, conquer, or bring under control
   Plantation owners *subjugated* their slaves and forced them to do manual labor.
   ant: free

6. **expedite** (ek´ spə dīt) *v.* to increase the rate of progress
   More construction workers were brought on to the project to help *expedite* the construction of the new bridge.
   syn: hurry; hasten; streamline *ant: retard; hinder*

7. **filibuster** (fil´ ə bəs tər) *v.* to attempt to block a bill from becoming law by speaking at length against it
   The Senator from Mississippi gave an eight-hour speech to *filibuster* the new tax bill.
   syn: derail

8. **pristine** (pris´ tēn) *adj.* pure; completely clean and uncontaminated
   The vast, *pristine* wilderness of northern Alaska is too cold and remote for most people to inhabit.
   syn: pure *ant: defiled; spoiled; sullied*

9. **pithy** (pi´ thē) *adj.* full of meaning; concise
The *pithy* statements in greeting cards are often short and sweet.
syn: succinct *ant: verbose*

10. **invective** (in vek´ tiv) *n.* an insult or abuse in speech
Scott's *invective*, aimed at his teacher, resulted in an immediate trip to the principal's office.
syn: reproach *ant: praise*

11. **prodigal** (prä´ di gəl) *adj.* reckless, wasteful, and extravagant
The *prodigal* actor was notorious for his lavish, excessive, and unruly lifestyle.
syn: wastrel; libertine *ant: prudent*

12. **pliable** (plī´ ə bəl) *adj.* easily bent or flexible
NASA had to devise a new, more *pliable* spacesuit for astronauts working on the the space station.
ant: rigid

13. **torpid** (tōr´ ped) *adj.* losing motion, feeling, or power; lacking in energy
The sleeping gas caused the hero's mind to become *torpid.*
syn: apathetic; lethargic *ant: energetic*

14. **tenuous** (ten´ yə wəs) *adj.* not dense or thick; having little substance
Even though it was published, the dissertation put forth a very tenuous theory on intelligence.
syn: thin; unconvincing; fragile *ant: strong; cogent*

15. **discordant** (dis kōrd´ dənt) *adj.* being in disagreement
The angry and *discordant* voices echoed throughout the conference room.
syn: conflicting *ant: harmonious*

EXERCISE I—Words in Context

From the list below, supply the words needed to complete the paragraph. Some words will not be used.

pristine	**discordant**	**xenophobia**	**subjugate**
impregnable	**invective**	**pithy**	**inherent**

A. Queen Alana's __________ was not entirely unfounded. In the queen's twenty-year reign, her lands had been the victim of four separate invasions, two of which nearly __________ the tiny island to foreign rule. The enemies had already expressed views __________ with the Queen's about their common borders. After issuing a fiery __________ questioning the foreign king's intentions, Queen Alana began to prepare for war. Two days later, the __________, old-world forest on the southern shore of her realm became crowded with invading troops, all of whom were preparing for an onslaught on the supposedly __________ castle.

From the list below, supply the words needed to complete the paragraph. Some words will not be used.

irreverent	**filibuster**	**prodigal**	**torpid**
inherent	**expedite**	**pithy**	**tenuous**

B. Despite four thousand years of erosion, the hieroglyphics on the wall still carried a[n] __________ message: "enter and be doomed." Murdoch, trying to __________ the heist, paid no attention to the symbols as he raised his pickaxe over his head and sent it crashing into the limestone wall. The native guide scolded Murdoch's __________ treatment of the ancient burial chamber, but Murdoch retorted with the quick explanation that etiquette was not a[n] __________ part of archaeological theft. Murdoch took a second swing, this time penetrating the surprisingly __________ wall. He grinned at the thought of what waited for him beyond the wall, unaware that the guide had become pale and stood in __________ amazement next to the catacomb entrance.

From the list below, supply the words needed to complete the paragraph. Some words will not be used.

filibuster	**prodigal**	**pliable**
xenophobia	**torpid**	**invective**

C. Senator Melita Darnell knew that she would have to __________ to prevent a vote on the new McDermid Bill. To her, the bill would pave the way for the same __________ government spending that she had vowed to eliminate; unfortunately, the opinions of the quorum were not _________ enough for her to sway prior to the session. She was going to have to do this the hard way.

EXERCISE II— Sentence Completion

Complete the sentence in a way that shows you understand the meaning of the italicized vocabulary word.

1. The car collector could tell by the *pristine* condition of the coupe that...

2. The *prodigal* lifestyle of the twin sisters caused the family to...

3. Many of the laborers became *torpid* when the weather...

4. The surgeon called from Nebraska to tell the Maryland courier to *expedite* the...

5. The advertising department sought a *pithy* catchphrase for...

6. *Discordant* union members were blamed for lost work during the...

7. Owing to unfounded *xenophobia*, some citizens fear...

8. The riotous soccer crowd was impossible to *subjugate* because...

9. The *impregnable* underground base proved to be impossible to...

10. *Pliable* eyeglass frames prevent the wearer from accidentally...

11. An *inherent* part of an automobile is the...

12. The *tenuous* criticism of the show did not...

13. The representative's *filibuster* prevented Congress from...

14. Irene's loud *invective* to Jye caused everyone within earshot to...

15. The mourners thought that Niles was *irreverent* to talk on his cell phone during...

EXERCISE III—Roots, Prefixes, and Suffixes

Study the entries and answer the questions that follow.

The roots *luc, lus, and lum* mean "light."
The prefix *il* means "in."
The root *ten* means "to hold."
The roots *cur* and *cours* mean "to run" or "to go."

A. Using literal translations as guidance, define the following words without using a dictionary:

1. illuminate
2. curriculum
3. tenet
4. current
5. tenant
6. luminosity

B. The root *lieu* means "place," so the literal translation of *lieutenant* is ______________________________.
If you deliver packages for people by running them from one place to another, your job title might be ____________________.

C. If *trans* means "through," then *translucent* means ____________________.
If you prefer a particular brand of bread, then you probably have a[n] ____________________ to purchase that brand when you go shopping.

D. List all the words you can think of that contain the roots *lus, luc,* or *ten.*

E. List all the words you can think of that contain the roots *cur* or *cours.*

EXERCISE IV—Inference

Complete the sentences by inferring information about the italicized word from its context.

A. The security company told Iniko that his house was *impregnable*, so he was surprised when he got home and discovered that…

B. If a senator *filibusters* a bill to enact a pay increase for congressmen, the other senators might tell her…

C. When you hear one driver shout *invectives* at another driver, you might assume that…

EXERCISE V—Critical Reading

Below is a pair of reading passages followed by several multiple-choice questions similar to the ones you will encounter on the SAT. Carefully read both passages and choose the best answer to each of the questions.

The following pair of passages presents two views on the issue of trying juvenile offenders as adults. Read the two passages and note the opposing views expressed by the two authors.

Passage 1

Our society cannot expect youths to be as responsible for their actions as adults. They have not lived long enough to learn all they need to know to determine right from wrong and to understand the consequences of their actions. When they are tried as adults and sentenced to jail, they do not receive the rehabilitation they need, and their chances for a proper education dissolve.

Juveniles do not experience rehabilitation by spending jail time in in adult populations. Tried as juveniles, they can receive essential treatment and social services in a juvenile center. They would learn why it was wrong to commit the crime and how to achieve better things with their lives. In prison, their education is all but finished because of a lack of schooling and the unlikelihood that they will return to school once they are released from jail; however, juveniles do receive some education in jail—education that is detrimental to their own well being and to the best interests of society. They learn from skilled criminals who are also in jail. Their new education exposes them to criminal tactics and new crimes to commit when the institution releases them, placing everyone in jeopardy.

The hard-time curriculum benefits no one; it is in the best interest of all people that young offenders be tried in a juvenile court where they can receive the rehabilitation and the education that they need to steer themselves away from troublemaking influences.

Passage 2

Trying juveniles as adults should be standard judicial practice in America. If the juvenile has committed a crime worthy of jail time, he will benefit as well as the American people. While in jail, juveniles acquire respect for their elders and realize the importance of freedom. If courts send them to jail once, juveniles will be less likely to commit a second criminal act that will send them back again. Also, if juveniles are not sentenced as adults, they get a free ride, learn a criminal lifestyle, and face a reverse form of age discrimination.

Undoubtedly, juveniles receive a free ride when handled in the juvenile court system. When juveniles commit a first offense of, for example, attempted murder, the courts usually parole them, giving them a second chance, even though they probably don't deserve it.

In addition, juvenile courts clear delinquents' records when youths reach eighteen years of age. No matter how many previous crimes, or the severity of the crimes, the courts still clear juvenile records as though nothing had happened. The system allows the habitual criminal to start a new life of crime with absolutely no previous record, no prior arrests or convictions to indicate that the adult offender needs to be treated differently from a person who is in trouble for the first time. This impotent system actually enables career criminals to continue their offensive lifestyles—it even encourages them to do it.

Persistent inaction of courts promotes lifestyles of habitual crime. Juveniles can't take a system seriously after that system repeatedly threatens to send them to jail. The more unpunished crimes these juvenile offenders commit, the less likely they are to expect any consequences.

Certainly, most courts think that juveniles are incapable of committing vicious crimes. Courts believe that a thirteen- or fourteen-year-old does not have the mental capability to commit murder. They assume that juveniles do not understand the consequences of pulling a trigger on a gun or stabbing someone. Courts can't presume that all juveniles have the same mental capability. Most thirteen- and fourteen-year-olds are indeed conscious of the crimes they commit. They do comprehend the results of pulling the trigger. The courts simply do not recognize the intelligence of youths. In addition, juries also show overwhelming sympathy for teens. Juries are hesitant to sentence juveniles to jail because they might not survive the harsh environment. Juries do not understand that if juveniles can commit the crime, they are strong enough to "do the time." Juveniles can withstand more than society realizes; they are facing age discrimination in courts.

When courts put juveniles back on the streets, they hurt us and our families. We don't want to put up with it anymore; we want action, and we want it now. Courts should try juveniles as adults and save the general population from their criminal acts.

1. The overall tone of the first passage is
   A. sympathetic.
   B. condemning.
   C. ironic.
   D. objective.
   E. demeaning.

2. What is the best paraphrase of the sentence, "They have not lived long enough to learn all they need to know to determine right from wrong and to understand the consequences of their actions" (passage 1, paragraph 1)?
   A. They are not smart.
   B. They are ignorant.
   C. They haven't lived life yet.
   D. They will never know what is right or wrong.
   E. They are inexperienced.

3. As used in the last sentence of passage 1, paragraph 1, the word *proper* most likely means
   A. peculiar.
   B. absolute.
   C. virtuous.
   D. genteel.
   E. traditional.

4. The overall tone of the second passage is
   A. sympathetic.
   B. ironic.
   C. objective.
   D. demeaning.
   E. critical.

5. As used in the second passage, the phrase *free ride* most likely means
   A. processing through the court system.
   B. attorney representation at taxpayer expense.
   C. tours of prison facilities.
   D. transportation from jail to court.
   E. activity without consequences.

6. Which of the following is *not* a type of age discrimination suggested by passage 2?
   A. Juveniles are not capable of committing vicious crimes.
   B. Juveniles do not have the mental capability for murder.
   C. Juveniles do not understand the consequences.
   D. Juveniles are conscious of the crimes they commit.
   E. Juveniles might not survive the harsh environment of jail.

7. The last paragraph of passage 2 evokes what sentiment in the reader?
   A. sympathy
   B. enthusiasm
   C. action
   D. regret
   E. interest

8. According to passage 2, which result occurs when juveniles are tried as adults?
   A. experience age discrimination
   B. a new life of crime
   C. earn a free ride
   D. gain respect of elders
   E. become rehabilitated

9. The primary difference between the two passages is that
   A. they present two opposing views on the same issue.
   B. passage 1 reports on the issue, while passage 2 analyzes it.
   C. passage 2 uses facts, while passage 1 merely uses generalities.
   D. each passage blames the court system.
   E. each passage contradicts the other on key facts.

10. The arguments of both passages are based on
    A. unsupported personal opinion.
    B. documented facts and statistics.
    C. personal opinion and case studies.
    D. eyewitness accounts.
    E. personal experience.

Lesson Nineteen

1. **mellifluous** (mə li´ flōō wəs) *adj.* having a rich, smoothly flowing sound
   The singer's *mellifluous* voice contributed to the relaxed atmosphere of the lounge.
   syn: harmonious *ant: strident; discordant*

2. **epicurean** (e pi kyū´ rē ən) *adj.* taking pleasure in food and drink
   The *epicurean* chef taught his students not only how to cook food, but also how to enjoy it.
   syn: hedonistic; gourmet

3. **oeuvre** (ë´ vrə **or** ōō vrə) *n.* the complete work of an artist, composer, or writer
   Shakespeare's *oeuvre* is one of the most respected groups of literary works ever written.
   syn: canon

4. **arbiter** (är´ bə tər) *n.* a person with the ability to resolve a disagreement; a judge
   The principal ended the conflict by acting as an *arbiter* between the two angry students.

5. **verdant** (vər´ dənt) *adj.* fresh and green, referring to plant life
   The *verdant* landscape reminded the O'Connells of their native Ireland so much that they decided to build a home there.
   syn: lush *ant: arid; sere*

6. **vagary** (vā´ gə rē) *n.* unpredictable action or behavior
   Kristin's *vagaries* prevented her from holding a job as an air traffic controller.
   syn: whim; caprice

7. **vacuous** (va´ kyə wəs) *adj.* lacking intelligence
   The student's *vacuous* expression revealed his failure to study for the test.
   syn: empty-headed *ant: brilliant; shrewd*

8. **attrition** (ə tri´ shən) *n.* a wearing down over time
   The company faced a severe *attrition* of its stock price because of bad publicity.
   syn: erosion *ant: buildup; accretion*

9. **archetype** (är´ ki tīp) *n.* a prototype or original model
   The *archetype* for the first airplane was only a toy model, but it has led to modern jets and supersonic fighter planes.
   syn: model *ant: product*

10. **approbation** (a prə bā´ shən) *n.* formal approval of an act
The president gave his *approbation* for the rescue of ten citizens who were being held hostage at a foreign embassy.
syn: authorization *ant: disapproval; opprobrium*

11. **burgeon** (bər´ jən) *v.* to grow, expand, or bloom
Increased colonization caused the island city to *burgeon.*
syn: swell *ant: shrink; diminish*

12. **commensurate** (kə men´ sər it) *adj.* an equal measure; corresponding in size and measurement
Though Margie and Liz attended different universities, they received *commensurate* educations.
syn: equivalent; comparable *ant: unequal*

13. **confluence** (kän´ flōō ənts) *n.* a meeting or gathering together
The United Nations General Assembly is a *confluence* of world thought.
syn: convergence; concourse *ant: divergence*

14. **coup** (kōō) *n.* a surprising, brilliant, and usually successful act
The rebels planned a *coup* to overthrow the current Prime Minister and install a new leader.
syn: plot

15. **secular** (se´ kyə lər) *adj.* not spiritual or religious; worldly
Many religions warn of the dangers of the *secular* world because they believe it is full of sin.
syn: earthly *ant: religious*

EXERCISE I—Words in Context

From the list below, supply the words needed to complete the paragraph. Some words will not be used.

arbiter vacuous burgeon commensurate vagary secular

A. As the terrorist threat __________ each year in the United States, citizens must raise their vigilance to __________ levels. Citizens must also hinder terrorist intelligence-gathering capabilities by implementing small irregularities in their day-to-day routines. This intentional __________ will prevent terrorists from determining the best time to attack. We must learn to vary concentrations of people, control the distribution of work schedules, and otherwise keep terrorists as __________ as possible about our daily routines.

From the list below, supply the words needed to complete the paragraph. Some words will not be used.

archetype	**verdant**	**attrition**	**confluence**
epicurean	**mellifluous**	**coup**	

B. Tonia closed her eyes to concentrate better on the __________ sounds of the mambo orchestra playing at Anconia's Night Club. She heard only what emanated through the wall behind the dumpster. She would stand next to the wall, close her eyes, and imagine that she was a member of the __________ clientele feasting at the glass tables in Anconia's impressive ballroom. Just a week before being hired, Tonia met Anconia's doorman after the club had closed for the night, and he was nice enough to allow her inside for a look. The walls around the dance floor and dining area were __________ with dangling, subtropical plants, and the dance floor sparkled even though the club was fifty years old. Impressed, Tonia realized how Anconia's provided a place for the __________ of the wealthy and the famous.

From the list below, supply the words needed to complete the paragraph. Some words will not be used.

oeuvre	**arbiter**	**attrition**	**archetype**
approbation	**coup**	**secular**	**vagary**

C. Many fans usually classified Toby as fitting the __________ of the traditional 1970s folksinger, but they were only partially correct. Toby's taste in Native American clothing and his simple, naturalist philosophical claims definitely gave him the "Woodstock" image. The music of his __________ was rich with naturalist and even spiritual themes, though it remained surprisingly __________. It certainly caught Toby's fans off-guard when he gave his __________ to allow the state of Alaska to drill for oil on his pristine, 4,500-acre property. Feeling used, Toby's fans abandoned their prevailing 1970s attitudes to stage a[n] __________ and bring Toby to his senses. Willow Records, Toby's recording company, had to employ a legion of __________ to restore relations with angry music distributors who faced a massive __________ of their revenues.

EXERCISE II—Sentence Completion

Complete the sentence in a way that shows you understand the meaning of the italicized vocabulary word.

1. Before taking the case to court, the companies brought in an *arbiter* to…

2. The *epicurean* restaurant owner paled when her doctor told her that…

3. To prove that he was not as *vacuous* as everyone thought, Gene…

4. Bonnie and Doug opted for a *secular* wedding because…

5. If the deadly bacteria in the dish *burgeon* uncontrollably, the scientist will…

6. The *confluence* of the rivers enabled…

7. Roslyn found it easy drift off to the *mellifluous* sounds of…

8. Tycho's *verdant* front yard resembled a tropical…

9. Picasso's *oeuvre* was the topic of conversation…

10. Unlike the traditional *archetype* of the mad scientist, Hans looks and behaves more like…

11. The vice-president of the corporation gave his *approbation* to finance the…

12. Had the *coup* failed, the country now known as the United States would be called…

13. Though Kaneka and Robin grew up in different places, they had *commensurate* levels of…

14. The *vagaries* and unpredictability of the hurricane…

15. The increase in student *attrition* in the advanced class caused…

EXERCISE III—Roots, Prefixes, and Suffixes

Study the entries and answer the questions that follow.

The root *cogn* means "to know."
The root *ped* means "foot."
The root *ject* means "to throw."
The prefix *inter* means "between"
The prefix *in* means "not."
The prefix *de* means "down."
The prefix *im* means "on, against."

A. *Using literal translations as guidance, define the following words without using a dictionary:*

1. interject
2. incognito
3. dejected
4. impediment
5. pedestrian
6. cognitive

B. If you need foot surgery, you will probably go to a[n] ____________________.

An insect that seems to have a thousand legs is called a[n] ____________________.

C. Bullets, arrows, and rocks thrown from catapults are types of ______________.

If *pro* means "before," then a *prognosis* is knowledge about __________________.

D. List all the words that you can think of that contain the roots *cogn*, *ped*, and *ject*.

EXERCISE IV—Inference

Complete the sentences by inferring information about the italicized word from its context.

A. If your front lawn becomes too *verdant*, your neighbors might tell you...

B. One explanation for the *confluence* of pigeons and robins on the street is...

C. A good reason for peasants to organize a *coup* against their president is...

EXERCISE V—Writing

Here is a writing prompt similar to the one you will find on the writing portion of the SAT.

Plan and write an essay based on the following statement:

> "Those who write clearly have readers, those who write obscurely have commentators."
>
> – Albert Camus

Assignment: Write an essay in which you explain what Camus means. Discuss his attitude toward writers and readers, and then, using evidence from your reading, your studies, and your observations, illustrate your opinion of his assertion.

Thesis: Write a *one-sentence* response to the above assignment. Make certain this single sentence offers a clear statement of your position.
Example: Albert Camus asserts that writers create certain types of readers, but in reality, each reader has a unique response that is not wholly determined by the clarity or the obscurity of the writing.

Organizational Plan: If your thesis is the point on which you want to end, where does your essay need to begin? List the points of development that are inevitable in leading your reader from your beginning point to your end point. This list is your outline.

Draft: Use your thesis as both your beginning and your end. Following your outline, write a good first draft of your essay. Remember to support all your points with examples, facts, references to reading, etc.

Review and Revise: Exchange essays with a classmate. Using the Holistic Scoring Guide on page 210, score your partner's essay (while he or she scores yours). If necessary, rewrite your essay to correct the problems indicated by the essay's score.

Improving Paragraphs

Read the following passage and then answer the multiple-choice questions that follow. Note that the questions will require you to make decisions regarding the revision of the reading selection.

(1) In 1891, Jay Gould, a wealthy railroad magnate, promised to rebuild a church in Roxbury, New York. (2) As a member of the church he had vowed to build, Gould knew that the previous building had been prone to storms and fires, he pledged to fund stone construction of the church, which is what had recently destroyed the church. (3) Never getting to see the church that was built with his money by his children, he died in 1892, but the church that Gould promised definitely was built.

(4) The church just happened to be erected right next to a house that had been built 30 years earlier, and one that Gould's daughter, Helen, fancied. (5) Not long after the church was completed, Helen bought the estate and named it "Kirkside" for its position adjacent to the neighboring Kirkside Lake. (6) The house was built by Liberty Preston.

(7) After Gould's death, his six children took up the cause and even financed the project. (8) Construction began in 1893 for the early English Gothic-style church built with rough-faced St. Lawrence marble. (9) In 1894, the dedication of the building honored Jay Gould, and the structure was named for him.

(10) When Helen died in 1938, the beauty of Kirkside became available to many other people. (11) Twelve acres of the estate have since become Kirkside Park, a center of activity in Roxbury. (12) Helen's brother donated the house to the Reformed Church of America as a retirement home for clerics and their families. (13) Eventually, the home was opened to elderly persons of all denominations.

1. To improve paragraph 1, sentence 2 should be
   A. deleted.
   B. broken into two sentences.
   C. moved to follow sentence 3.
   D. combined with sentences 1 and 2.
   E. left unchanged.

2. Choose the best revision of sentence 3.
   A. Gould died in 1892, long before the project was finished, but his children ensured that his promise went fulfilled.
   B. Before dying in 1892, Gould did not get to see the church built, though his children did, using their inheritance.
   C. The church was not built before Gould died in 1892, but his children used his money for the same purpose.
   D. Before his promise was fulfilled, Gould died, and, in 1892, his children rebuilt the church.
   E. When Gould died in 1892, the church could not be rebuilt unless Gould's children continued the project, which they did happily, though Gould did not get to see the final product.

3. Which of the following suggestions would improve the organization of the passage?
   A. Exchange paragraph 4 with paragraph 2.
   B. Exchange paragraph 3 with paragraph 1.
   C. Exchange paragraph 4 with paragraph 3.
   D. Exchange paragraph 1 with paragraph 4.
   E. Exchange paragraph 3 with paragraph 2.

4. Which sentence could be deleted without changing the intent of the passage?
   A. Sentence 4
   B. Sentence 5
   C. Sentence 6
   D. Sentence 7
   E. Sentence 8

5. Choose the most appropriate title for the passage.
   A. Two Parks for the Price of One
   B. Legacy of a Robber Baron
   C. Jay Gould's Kirkside Home
   D. The Gift of Gould
   E. Children of Wealth

Lesson Twenty

1. **insouciant** (in sōō´ sē ənt) *adj.* not concerned; free from care
   Jenna's *insouciant* attitude made her easy to befriend.
   syn: nonchalant *ant: worried*

2. **static** (sta´ tik) *adj.* without force or movement; stationary
   The old truck remained *static* in the front yard because it was out of gasoline.
   syn: immobile; inert *ant: dynamic*

3. **stipulate** (sti´ pyə lāt) *v.* to specify a required part of an agreement
   The developer *stipulated* that before construction could begin, the homeowners must first provide a down payment.
   syn: require

4. **zeitgeist** (zīt´ gīst) *n.* the general spirit of the time
   Some consider the *zeitgeist* of the 1960s to be one of moral decay, while others see it as a time of reform.

5. **proliferate** (prə li´ fə rāt) *v.* to grow or reproduce rapidly
   The plant food enabled Bob's irises to *proliferate* throughout the flower bed.
   syn: multiply *ant: diminish*

6. **tenet** (te´ nət) *n.* a belief or principle held to be true
   Belief in the Holy Trinity is one of the main *tenets* of Christianity.
   syn: cornerstone; creed

7. **ruminate** (rōō´ mə nāt) *v.* to think deeply or repeatedly
   The great philosopher could often be found *ruminating* over the questions of humanity.
   syn: ponder; reflect

8. **vigilant** (vi´ jə lent) *adj.* alert at all times; watchful
   The family's watchdog remained *vigilant* during the day, but he fell into a deep sleep at night.
   syn: alert *ant: oblivious*

9. **dissident** (di´ sə dənt) *n.* someone who disagrees
   The *dissidents* of the proposed welfare bill staged a protest.
   syn: renegade *ant: supporter*

10. **petulant** (pe´ chə lənt) *adj.* rude in speech or behavior; peevish
    Mike's *petulant* remarks toward his boss earned him a demotion and a cut in pay.
    syn: contemptuous *ant: original*

11. **derivative** (də ri´ və tiv) *n.* not the original; coming from another source
    The modern English word "engine" is a *derivative* of the Latin word "ingenium."
    syn: offspring; branch

12. **accolade** (a´ kə lād) *n.* an award or honor
    The reporter received *accolades* for her newest article that uncovered a serious money-laundering scandal.
    syn: kudos; recognition *ant: opprobrium*

13. **demur** (di mər´) *v.* to disapprove or to take exception
    Martin *demurred* when Sandy suggested that they spend Friday evening at the ballet.
    syn: object; disagree *ant: agree; acquiesce*

14. **limpid** (lim´ pəd) *adj.* transparent; clear
    The warm, *limpid* waters of the Aegean Sea provide excellent snorkeling opportunities.
    ant: murky

15. **invidious** (in vi´ dē əs) *adj.* tending to cause discontent, harm, or resentment; offensively unfair
    The *invidious* book caused a huge controversy over implications that a leading presidential candidate committed a crime.
    syn: malicious *ant: conciliatory*

EXERCISE I—Words in Context

From the list below, supply the words needed to complete the paragraph. Some words will not be used.

limpid	**proliferate**	**tenet**	**ruminate**	**accolade**
zeitgeist	**stipulate**	**insouciant**	**static**	**dissident**

A. Thirty years of saving money finally paid off when Vernita found the cottage of her dreams on the coast of Maine—or so she thought. Despite a handful of local __________, the Clifftown Historical Society approved the sale of the property, but not before they __________ one important factor: the new owner must keep the windmill in operating condition because it had been a landmark of the town for generations. Shrugging off the windmill as a minor concern, Vernita seized the opportunity to purchase the lot. Six months later, Vernita learned why the __________ of the cottage's original era included a rigorous work ethic.

The problems began when she walked outside on a breezy morning and noticed the __________ blades of the windmill despite the considerable breeze. The shaft to the millstones had broken, and its repair required nearly two thousand dollars and three weeks of toiling for her and two paid workmen. Two days after completing the repairs, the well began to pump a muddy, undrinkable liquid instead of the usual cool, __________ spring water. While contractors dug a new well, Vernita discovered that mold and insects had __________ in the dank basement. The unending problems caused Vernita to __________ on why she had ever bought the house. She had always harbored the __________ that sometimes people just have to know when to quit, and Vernita also missed the __________ life that she had while renting someone else's property. Three months later, Vernita moved back into a condominium.

From the list below, supply the words needed to complete the paragraph. Some words will not be used.

static	**accolade**	**vigilant**	**petulant**
invidious	**demur**	**derivative**	**stipulate**

B. "Keep your __________ comments to yourself," said Kyle. "They're not going to help matters. We needed a pilot, and Brad was the only team member who even came close."

Lee Ann stopped complaining, but she thought again of how she originally __________ to Logan's half-witted escape plan: grab the canisters, sneak out of the compound, run through the jungle, and steal one of the two old cargo planes on the dirt runway. Two team members had already been wounded, and Brad wasn't about to win any __________ for his abilities to get the dilapidated machine off the ground.

"This plane's no good!" screamed Brad. "The left engine must need maintenance!"

"Let's try the other plane before the alarm sounds!" yelled Lee Ann. The team grabbed what little gear they had left, exited the plane, and hurried across the tarmac. Knowing that Benedito's security force would soon descend on them, the keen operatives remained __________ even as they scrambled to the other plane with their gear. While boarding, Kyle flinched when he looked beyond the flaps and caught the __________ sight of motorcycles entering the runway from the access road to the compound.

"Fire it up! Now!" yelled Kyle as he crawled over the team and landed with a thud in the primitive cockpit. "And check the canisters!"

Lee Ann checked. Luckily, the two quart-sized stainless steel canisters were intact and sealed; after all, one milligram of Prenitite would be more than enough to stop the hearts of everyone on the plane. A[n] __________ of the Prentonica seed, Prenitite was the number one item on every insane dictator's grocery list.

EXERCISE II—Sentence Completion

Complete the sentence in a way that shows you understand the meaning of the italicized vocabulary word.

1. My moral *tenets* prevent me from helping you to...
2. Your *petulant* attitude toward our clients has cost the company...
3. Displeased with the mayor's decision, several *dissidents*...
4. The tide pools are so *limpid* that you can see...
5. The reformists decided that the present *zeitgeist* did not...
6. The *vigilant* soldier on night watch heard the...
7. The *invidious* work of art was only displayed for one day before...
8. As landmines *proliferate*, special United Nations teams...
9. The mayor realized his mistake when the *insouciant* toll bridge operator...
10. Chloe received *accolades* for exposing the corporate cover-up, but then her boss...
11. I *demur* to being the first person to...
12. From the Greek root "chron," we get the *derivative* word...
13. If you *ruminate* too much before you swing the bat, you'll definitely...
14. I would have bought the car, but the dealer *stipulated* that...
15. Vaughn assumed that the *static* pendulum meant that the clock was...

EXERCISE III—Roots, Prefixes, and Suffixes

Study the entries and answer the questions that follow.

The roots *cord* and *card* mean "heart" or "mind."
The roots *quis* and *quir* mean "to seek."
The prefix *ac* means "towards."
The prefix *in* means "into."
The prefix *cata* means "down" or "thoroughly"
The root *tonia* means, "paralysis."
The root *clysm* means "flood, disaster."

A. *Using literal translations as guidance, define the following words without using a dictionary:*

1. inquisitive
2. discordant
3. acquisitive
4. catatonia
5. cataclysm
6. cordial

B. An agreement among nations to stop a particular behavior is sometimes called a[n] ______________________.
Explain why the word *catapult* would use the "to put down" form of *cata.*
Repeat the process for the word *catalog.*

C. The purpose of an *inquisition* is to ________________________________.
If the prefix *re* means "again," what is the literal translation of *record* (verb form)?

D. List as many words as you can that contain the roots *cord*, *quis*, or *cata.*

EXERCISE IV—Inference

Complete the sentences by inferring information about the italicized word from its context.

A. Though the nations are not at war, their weapons continue to *proliferate* because…

B. If the political *dissident* does not publicly retract his statement, the dictator might…

C. If the lake is no longer *limpid* after the factory begins production, you might assume that…

EXERCISE V—Critical Reading

From 1804 to 1806, Meriwether Lewis and William Clark led the first official overland expedition to the Pacific Coast. The following passages are Lewis and Clark's journal entries for April 20, 1806, about one month into the return trip. The expedition party is near the Columbia River, which forms the border between Washington and Oregon.

Passage 1

Sunday, April 20, 1806 (Captain Lewis):

Some frost this morning. The Eneeshur and Skilloots are much better clad than they were last fall; their men have generally leggings, moccasins, and large robes; many of them wear shirts of the same form with those of the Shoshone Chopunnish, highly ornamented with porcupine 5 quills. The dress of their women differs very little from those of the great rapids and above. Their children frequently wear robes of the large grey squirrel skins, those of the men and women are principally deer skins, some wolf, elk, bighorn, and buffalo; the latter they procure from the nations who sometimes visit the Missouri. Indeed a considerable 10 proportion of their wearing apparel is purchased from their neighbors to the northwest in exchange for pounded fish, copper, and beads. At present, the principal village of the Eneeshur is below the falls on the north side of the river. One other village is above the falls on the south side and another a few miles above on the north side. The first consists 15 of nineteen, the second of eleven, and the third of five lodges. Their houses, like those of the Skilloots, have their floors on the surface of the ground, but are formed of sticks and covered with mats and straw. They are large and contain usually several families each. For fuel, they use straw, small willows, and the southern wood. They use the silk grass 20 in manufacturing their fishing nets and bags, and the bear grass and cedar bark are employed in forming a variety of articles. They are poor, dirty, proud, haughty, inhospitable, parsimonious, and faithless in every respect; nothing but our numbers, I believe, prevents their attempting to murder us at this moment.

25 This morning I was informed that the natives had pilfered six tomahawks and a knife from the party in the course of the last night. I spoke to the chief on this subject. He appeared angry with his people and addressed them, but the property was not restored. One horse which I had purchased and paid for yesterday, and which could not be found 30 when I ordered the horses into close confinement yesterday, I was now informed had been gambled away by the rascal who had sold it to me and had been taken away by a man of another nation. I therefore took the goods back from this fellow. I purchased a gun from the chief for which I gave him two elk skins. In the course of the day, I obtained two 35 other indifferent horses for which I gave an extravagant price. I found that I should get no more horses and therefore resolved to proceed

tomorrow morning with those which I had and to convey the baggage in two small canoes that the horses could not carry. For this purpose, I had a load made up for seven horses; the eighth Bratton was compelled to
40 ride as he was yet unable to walk. I bartered my elk skins, old irons, and two canoes for beads. One of the canoes for which they would give us but little, I had cut up for fuel. These people have yet a large quantity of dried fish on hand, yet they will not let us have any but for an exorbitant price. We purchased two dogs and some shappellel from them. I had
45 the horses grazed until evening and then picketed and hobbled them within the limits of our camp. I ordered the indians from our camp this evening and informed them that if I caught them attempting to purloin any article from us, I would beat them severely. They went off in rather a bad humor, and I directed the party to examine their arms and be on
50 their guard. They stole two spoons from us in the course of the day. The Scaddals, Squan-nan-os, Shan-wah-purrs, and Shallattas reside to the northwest of these people, and depend on hunting deer and elk and trade with these people for their pounded fish.

Passage 2

Sunday, April 20, 1806 (Captain Clark):

This morning very cold; hills covered with snow. I showed the natives what I had to give for their horses and attempted to purchase them. They informed me that they would not sell any horses to me, that their horses were at a long ways off and they would not trade them. My
5 offer was a blue robe, a calico shirt, a handkerchief, five parcels of paint, a knife, a wampum moon, four braces of ribbon, a piece of brass, and about six braces of yellow beads; and to that amount for what I had, I also offered my large blue blanket for one, my coat, sword and plume—none of which seemed to entice those people to give horses if they had
10 any. They sat in their huts, which are mats supported on poles without fire. At night, when they wish a light, they burn dry straw and some small, dry willows. They speak different from those below, and have but little to eat. Some roots and dried fish are to be found in their houses. I am half frozen at this inhospitable village, which is moved from its posi-
15 tion above the falls to one below, and contains nineteen large houses. A village is also established on the other side, immediately above the falls. All the natives who were established above the falls for some distance have moved. Those people are much better dressed than they were at the time we went down the river. They have all new deer, elk, ibex, goat, and
20 wolf skin robes, their children have also the large squirrel skin robes. Many of them have leggings and moccasins, all of which they procure from the indians at a distance in exchange for their pounded fish and beads. They also purchase silk grass, of which they make their nets and sails for taking fish. They also purchase bear grass and many other things

25 for their fish. Those people gave me roots and berries prepared in different ways, for which I gave some small articles in return. Great numbers of skimming nets on their houses. Those people are poor and kind of dirty and indolent. They wear their hair loose and flowing; the men cut in the forward, which the Skilloots do not.

30 I could not procure a single horse from those people, during this day, at any price. They offered me two for two kettles, of which we could not spare. I used every artifice decent and even false statements to induce those poor devils to sell me horses. In the evening, two different men offered to sell me three horses, which they informed me were a little 35 distance off and they would bring them immediately. Those two persons, as I found, went immediately off up the river to their tribe without any intention to find or sell their horses. A little before sunset, three men arrived from some distance above and informed me that they came to see me. At sunset, finding no probability of Captain Lewis' arrival, I 40 packed up the articles and took them into the lodge in which I lay last night. Great numbers of those people gathered around me to smoke. I gave them two pipes and lay down in the back part of the house with Sgt. P. and the men with our arms situated as to be ready in case of any alarm. Those poor people appear entirely harmless—I purchased a dog 45 and some wood with a little pounded fish and shappellels. Made a fire on the rocks and cooked the dogs on which the men breakfasted and dined. Wind was hard all day, cold and from the northwest.

1. Lewis' party (passage 1) lacks enough horses to carry all the equipment, so Lewis
   A. hires Skilloots to help him carry the gear.
   B. burns anything that he cannot carry.
   C. purchases eight more horses.
   D. transports the equipment in canoes.
   E. purchases dogs to pull a sled.

2. According to passage 1, one horse does not carry equipment because
   A. the horse is unable to walk.
   B. it is Captain Bratton's expensive show horse.
   C. the equipment is placed in canoes.
   D. the horse is stubborn and refuses to cross the river.
   E. it must carry Bratton, an injured member of the party.

3. As used in line 45, *hobbled* most nearly means
   A. limped.
   B. broke the legs of to prevent escape.
   C. allowed to graze for food.
   D. tied the legs of to restrict movement.
   E. staggered, as though suffering from leg wounds.

4. Which information can be inferred from passage 2, paragraph 2?
   A. Lewis and Clark are lost somewhere near the Pacific coast.
   B. The natives treat Clark better than Lewis.
   C. Lewis and Clark were not together in the same camp.
   D. Clark successfully convinces the natives to sell horses.
   E. Lewis is waiting for Clark to arrive.

5. As used in line 32 of passage 2, *artifice* most nearly means
   A. an obvious lie.
   B. a crafty maneuver.
   C. currency.
   D. a threatening statement.
   E. a false promise.

6. To purchase clothing from other nations, the Eneeshur and Skilloot Indians used
   A. kettles.
   B. buffalo hides.
   C. shappellel.
   D. pounded fish.
   E. calico.

7. Which statement is false at the time the journal entries were written?
   A. Lewis and Clark had not previously met the Eneeshur and Skilloot Indians.
   B. One Eneeshur village contained nineteen lodges.
   C. The expedition teams needed horses.
   D. The expedition teams ate dogs.
   E. Porcupine quills were a valuable source of nutrition.

8. Lewis and Clark do not agree
   A. on the weather conditions.
   B. on the general physical appearance of the natives.
   C. that there is a need for more horses.
   D. on the level of threat posed by the natives.
   E. that the Eneeshur and Skilloots are fishermen.

9. Which choice best describes the difference in tone between the passages?
   A. Passage 2 is not as impersonal as passage 1.
   B. Passage 2 is more detached and impersonal than passage 1.
   C. Clark (passage 2) does not refer to himself in the first person.
   D. Clark (passage 2) is upset about the thefts, and Lewis (passage 1) is not.
   E. Passage 1 is spirited and lively, while passage 2 is serious and solemn.

10. In their journal entries, neither Lewis nor Clark mentions
    A. the location of the Shallatta Indians.
    B. the weather conditions.
    C. the locations of the Eneeshur villages.
    D. the characteristics of the native dwellings.
    E. the distance the party plans to travel the next day.

Lesson Twenty-One

1. **august** (o gəst´) *adj.* marked by grandeur and awe
The coronation of the queen was an *august* occasion that was full of pomp and circumstance.
syn: regal; magnificent *ant: pedestrian; common*

2. **ancillary** (an´ si lə rē) *adj.* subsidiary; providing assistance
The senior executive of the firm hired an *ancillary* worker to do his filing and typing.

3. **semblance** (sem´ bləns) *n.* an outward likeness in form or appearance
The suspect's alibi was only a partial *semblance* of the truth.
syn: similarity; copy

4. **autodidact** (o tō dī´ dakt) *n.* a self-taught person
With accomplishments in law, politics, and literature, Abe Lincoln is perhaps the most famous *autodidact* in American history.
syn: self-made

5. **asinine** (as´ ə nīn) *adj.* exhibiting poor judgment or intelligence
Jonah revealed his *asinine* tendencies when he rudely insulted the rabbi.
syn: foolish; boorish *ant: sagacious*

6. **albeit** (ôl bē´ ət) *conj.* although; even though
It was rainy and miserable all summer, *albeit* good for the crops.

7. **conduit** (kän´ dōō ət) *n.* a means by which something is transmitted
The telephone wire must be plugged into the *conduit* for the computer to connect to the Internet.
syn: channel

8. **philatelist** (fə lat´ əl ist) *n.* one who collects stamps
As a prominent *philatelist*, Dr. James has over ten thousand stamps in his collection.

9. **indefatigable** (in di fat´ i gə bəl) *adj.* tireless; incapable of being fatigued
Dave was so passionate about his work that he seemed almost *indefatigable* to the rest of the group.
ant: exhausted

10. **martyr** (mär´ tər) *n.* one who suffers or sacrifices for a cause
    Martin Luther King became a *martyr* for the civil rights movement when an assassin killed him.

11. **indiscretion** (in dis kresh´ ən) *n.* a minor misdeed
    If it is scandalous enough, a single *indiscretion* can cost a politician his or her career.
    syn: peccadillo; transgression

12. **osmosis** (äz mō´ səs) *n.* a gradual, often unconscious, process of absorption
    Living in a foreign country allowed Jerry to learn its language by *osmosis*.

13. **picayune** (pi kē yōōn´) *adj.* of very little value; trivial
    Mike's *picayune* collection of toy trucks had more sentimental value than the few dollars it would get at auction.
    syn: worthless; cheap *ant: valuable*

14. **dossier** (dos´ yā) *n.* a file of detailed information on a person or subject
    The police had a large *dossier* on the man accused of the theft.
    syn: record

15. **behest** (bi hest´) *n.* a command or urgent request
    Tyler grudgingly obeyed his mother's *behest* to come home early after the school dance.
    syn: demand

EXERCISE I—Words in Context

From the list below, supply the words needed to complete the paragraph. Some words will not be used.

dossier	**semblance**	**picayune**	**albeit**
august	**indefatigable**	**philatelist**	**behest**

A. Like many residents of Crystal Point, Janine walked to the beach every evening to witness the __________ beauty of the sun setting over the Pacific. The white dunes were the best place to experience the beautiful event, __________ several barges on the horizon diminished the view. They were a[n] __________ detail to Janine; it would require more than a few dots on the horizon to distract her from the blazing sky. Today, as Janine approached the water, she was amused to find a large mound of sand that had the vague __________ of a whale. The Williards must have visited the beach; they have three __________ children who readily spend entire days creating sand sculptures.

From the list below, supply the words needed to complete the paragraph. Some words will not be used.

asinine	**conduit**	**osmosis**	**august**
autodidact	**indiscretion**	**behest**	

B. Alicia knew that it was __________ to wait until the night before the deadline to write her term paper. Her teacher had accepted a late paper in the past, but such a(n) __________ could not ne ignored this time because it was the end of the grading period.

Luckily for her, Alicia was a(n) __________ who spent her free time reading about the subject of her paper. Having parents who were experts in the field also helped; raised by two historians, Alicia had learned more about history through __________ than she could ever hope to acquire in a classroom.

From the list below, supply the words needed to complete the paragraph. Some words will not be used.

conduit	**semblance**	**dossier**	**philatelist**
ancillary	**behest**	**martyr**	

C. At the FBI Director's __________, Special Agent Ford compiled a[n] __________ on Caroline Polk, including a list of charges, previous warrants, and a psychological profile. No, it was not every day that a stamp thief made it to the most-wanted list, but Polk had simply gone too far when she burglarized the stamp collection of Terry Moore, a well known __________ and, more important, a United States Senator. Identifying the suspect had taken only hours; thanks to some __________ guidance from the local police department's homicide unit, investigators found Polk's fingerprints all over the heating __________ that she used to enter the Senator's house. Polk's fingerprints were on record, largely because she was the only person in the country currently wanted for the grand theft of precious stamps. The Bureau had declined to arrest Polk in the past, for she was known to be armed, and few agents were willing to become __________ to the cause of stamp collecting.

EXERCISE II—Sentence Completion

Complete the sentence in a way that shows you understand the meaning of the italicized vocabulary word.

1. Ursula was reminded of her past *indiscretions* every time she...

2. "Your *dossier* reads like a novel," said Dr. Insano as he...

3. Your concerns are too *picayune* for me to...

4. The weather was sunny and clear, *albeit*...

5. If the hospital should suffer a blackout, there's an *ancillary* generator to...

6. Phoebe felt out of place at the *august* induction ceremony because...

7. The highlight of the *philatelist's* collection is a...

8. The broken underground gas *conduit* caused a mass...

9. Thanks to four cups of coffee, the *indefatigable* Elizabeth can finish...

10. Ivan was brave, but he wasn't about to become a *martyr* for...

11. At the Admiral's *behest*, Petty Officer Young gave the order to...

12. Audrey's *asinine* decision to put foil in the microwave resulted in...

13. As if by *osmosis*, the rambunctious hockey fans turned the docile Freddy...

14. Living far from civilization and schools, the *autodidact* had to...

15. The shoddy reality show didn't bear any *semblance* of...

EXERCISE III—Roots, Prefixes, and Suffixes

Study the entries and answer the questions that follow.

The roots *cap*, *capt*, *cept* and *cip* mean "to take" or "to seize."
The roots *grad* and *gress* mean "step" or "to go."
The prefix *inter* means "between," "among," or "in the presence of."

A. *Using literal translations as guidance, define the following words without using a dictionary:*

1. regress	4. precept
2. degrade	5. captivate
3. digress	6. capacious

B. Police will use their cars to ____________________ a driver who flees the scene of a crime.
If the prefix *e* means "out," then the literal translation for *egress* is ____________________.

C. The root *mit* means "to send." What is the appropriate word to describe a radio signal that fades in and out, causing periods of silence between audible transmissions?
The root *rog* means "to ask." What would you call a formal questioning of someone who is present, and expected, to answer the questions?

D. List all the words you can think of that contain the roots *cap, capt, cip,* or *cept.*

E. List all the words you can think of that begin with the prefix *inter.*

EXERCISE IV—Inference

Complete the sentences by inferring information about the italicized word from its context.

A. The FBI might compile a *dossier* on someone who…

B. If the *autodidact* did not have access to a library, she might not…

C. Since the *ancillary* forces failed to arrive in time, the battalion defending the fort…

EXERCISE V—Writing

Here is a writing prompt similar to the one you will find on the writing portion of the SAT.

Plan and write an essay based on the following statement:

> Some men see things as they are and say "Why?" I dream things that never were and say, "Why not?"
>
> – George Bernard Shaw

Assignment: Write an essay in which you explain George Bernard Shaw's quotation. What is implied in contrasting the two types of people? Be certain to illustrate and support all of your points with examples and evidence from your own reading, classroom studies, and personal observation and experience.

Thesis: Write a *one-sentence* response to the above assignment. Make certain this single sentence offers a clear statement of your position.
Example: George Bernard Shaw's quotation describes the difference between those people who understand and those who create, and both are necessary in the world.

Organizational Plan: If your thesis is the point on which you want to end, where does your essay need to begin? List the points of development that are inevitable in leading your reader from your beginning point to your end point. This list is your outline.

Draft: Use your thesis as both your beginning and your end. Following your outline, write a good first draft of your essay. Remember to support all your points with examples, facts, references to reading, etc.

Review and Revise: Exchange essays with a classmate. Using the Holistic Scoring Guide on page 210, score your partner's essay (while he or she scores yours). If necessary, rewrite your essay to correct the problems noted by your partner.

Identifying Sentence Errors

Identify the errors in the following sentences. If the sentence contains no error, select answer choice E.

1. Only a few (A) stars were visible last night, (B) because there was (C) a full moon (D). No error. (E)

2. By the time the hail started, (A) we had already (B) ran into (C) the library (D). No error. (E)

3. Radio stations aired the story (A) about the miracle operation (B) to restore sight to a blind man (C) in every region of the country (D). No error. (E)

4. Jane was already (A) for the prom (B) one hour before (C) her date arrived (D). No error. (E)

5. The university registrar (A) is responsible for scheduling office staff, (B) coordinating the directory of classes (C) and examinations, and assigning classroom facilities (D). No error. (E)

Improving Sentences

The underlined portion of each sentence below contains some flaw. Select the answer that best corrects the flaw.

6. Julie added vegetables to the stew, and then it simmered for 20 minutes before she served it.
   A. and then she allowed it to simmer
   B. simmered
   C. before it simmered
   D. simmered and stirred
   E. having chopped them first

7. On Christmas morning, the children had almost opened all their gifts by 6 am.
   A. had opened almost all their gifts
   B. had almost unwrapped all their gifts
   C. had unwrapped all their gifts
   D. had almost opened some presents
   E. had opened all their gifts

8. New research shows that high I.Q. scores are the result of heredity and also an intellectually stimulating environment.
   A. heredity and an intellectually stimulating environment.
   B. heredity and environments that are intellectually stimulating.
   C. genes and also intellectual stimulation.
   D. genes and environment.
   E. heredity and also environmental causes.

9. Mary told Ellen that she would need a new outfit to wear to the job interview.
   A. Mary told herself that she would need
   B. Mary told Ellen that she needed
   C. Mary told Ellen that she was going to need
   D. Mary told Ellen, "You will need…"
   E. Mary did not tell Ellen that she would need

10. Neither Anthony nor Rose like the beach.
    A. care for the beach
    B. cares for the beach
    C. likes the beach
    D. likes to go to the beach
    E. Ralph like the beach

REVIEW

Lessons 15 – 21

EXERCISE I – Sentence Completion

Choose the best pair of words to complete the sentence. Most choices will fit grammatically and will even make sense logically, but you must choose the pair that best fits the idea of the sentence.

Note that these words are not taken directly from lessons in this book. This exercise is intended to replicate the sentence completion portion of the SAT.

1. The lawyer argued that while his client might actually have been _________ at the burglary, she certainly was not a major _____________.
   A. aware, thief
   B. shocked, victim
   C. present, participant
   D. seen, conspirator
   E. there, collaborator

2. One employee __________ company security by illegally obtaining a badge that __________ him access to top secret offices.
   A. plagued, promised
   B. reduced, allowed
   C. stagnated, granted
   D. ridiculed, introduced
   E. compromised, afforded

3. The mayor wanted to _____________ the voting, and he ____________ those on his staff who still insisted on using complex and discriminatory rules for registering.
   A. facilitate, admonished
   B. speed, sought
   C. lengthen, blamed
   D. refine, reprimanded
   E. calcify, hired

4. The __________ amount of rain that fell on the edges of the Sahara made caravan travel there nearly __________ that year.
   A. quantity, foolish
   B. copious, avoidable
   C. vast, impossible
   D. marvelous, normal
   E. regular, impassable

5. The __________ with which the debaters defended their opposing views led many in the audience to believe that there might actually be a physical __________.
   A. lucidity, apology
   B. tenacity, altercation
   C. complexity, disagreement
   D. facts, confrontation
   E. solemnity, reconciliation

6. After a somber reevaluation, it became __________ clear to Albert that the way he had treated the elderly man was __________.
   A. abundantly, reprehensible
   B. horribly, adequate
   C. manifestly, proper
   D. quite, justified
   E. nearly, immaterial

7. The Wright brothers' problems with the early __________ of their plane almost made them __________ their plans to develop it.
   A. models, hasten
   B. demonstrations, delay
   C. designs, surpass
   D. flights, supplant
   E. prototypes, scrap

8. The translation of the book into Spanish was very __________ done, and most readers were __________ by its meaning.
   A. ineptly, perplexed
   B. expertly, confused
   C. succinctly, relieved
   D. rapidly, astounded
   E. professionally, confounded

EXERCISE II – Crossword Puzzle

Use the clues to complete the crossword puzzle. The answers consist of vocabulary words from lessons 15 through 21.

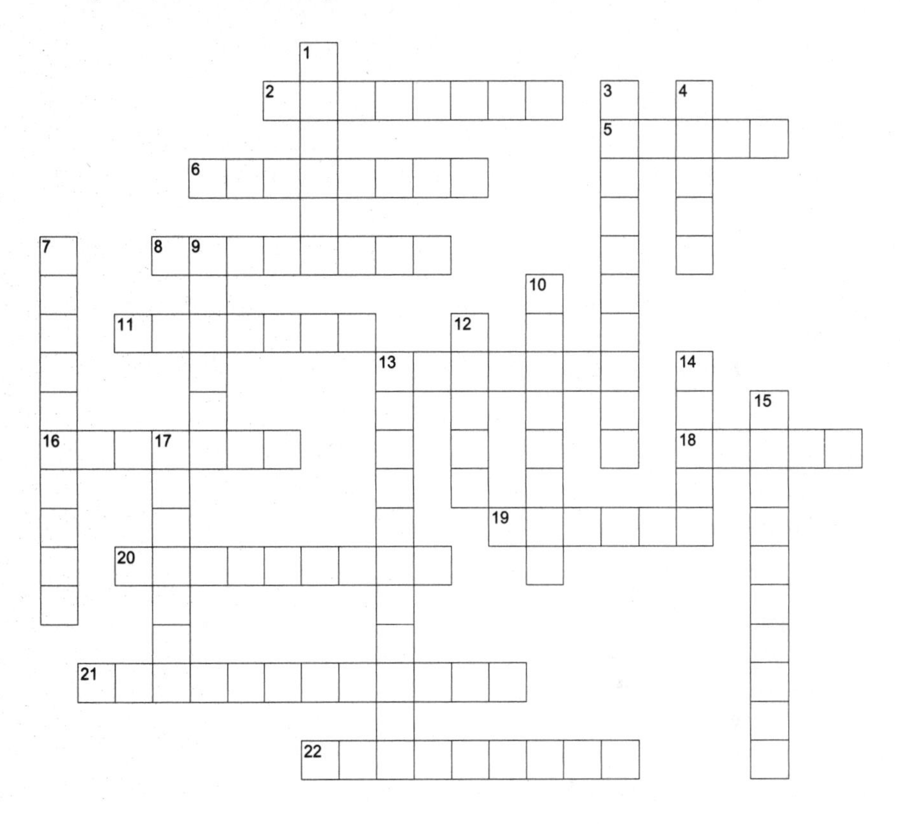

Across
2. ponder
5. hatred
6. rude
8. quiet
11. mediator
13. to steal
16. sarcastic
18. succinct
19. whim
20. to dominate
21. stingy
22. wearing away

Down
1. stately
3. gathering place
4. to displease
7. carefree
9. although
10. wasteful
12. tasteless
13. stamp collector
14. concise
15. advanced
17. not religious

Scoring Guide for the SAT Writing Test

ORGANIZATION

6 = Clearly Competent

The paper is clearly **organized** around the central point or main idea.
The work is **free of surface errors** (grammar, spelling, punctuation, etc.).

5 = Reasonably Competent

The **organizational plan** of the paper is **clear, but not fully implemented.**
Minor surface errors are present, but they **do not interfere** with the reader's understanding of the work.

4 = Adequately Competent

The **organizational plan** of the paper is **apparent, but not consistently implemented.**
Surface errors are present, but they **do not severely interfere** with the reader's understanding.

3 = Nearly Competent

There is evidence of an **organizational plan**.
Surface errors are **apparent** and **begin to interfere** with the reader's understanding of the work.

2 = Marginally Incompetent

The **organizational plan** of the writing is obscured by **too few** details and/or **irrelevant** details.
Surface errors are **frequent and severe enough** to **interfere** with the reader's understanding of the work.

1 = Incompetent

There is **no clear organizational plan** and/or **insufficient material**.
Surface errors are **frequent** and **extreme**, and **severely interfere** with the reader's understanding of the work.

Scoring Guide for the SAT Writing Test

DEVELOPMENT

6 = Clearly Competent

There is **sufficient** material (details, examples, anecdotes, supporting facts, etc.) to allow the reader to feel he/she has read a full and complete discussion without notable gaps, unanswered questions, or unexplored territory in the topic. Every word, phrase, clause, and sentence is **relevant**, contributing effectively to the thesis.

The work is **free of surface errors** (grammar, spelling, punctuation, etc.).

5 = Reasonably Competent

There is **nearly sufficient** material for a full and complete discussion, but the reader is left with **a few unanswered questions.** There is no superfluous or **irrelevant** material.

Minor surface errors are present, but they **do not interfere** with the reader's understanding of the work.

4 = Adequately Competent

There is **nearly sufficient** material for a full and complete discussion, but the reader is left with **a few unanswered questions.** Irrelevant material is present.

Surface errors are present, but they **do not severely interfere** with the reader's understanding.

3 = Nearly Competent

There is evidence of an organizational plan. There are **too few** details, examples, anecdotes, supporting facts, etc.

Surface errors are **apparent** and **begin to interfere** with the reader's understanding of the work.

2 = Marginally Incompetent

The organizational plan of the writing is obscured by **too few** details and/or **irrelevant** details.

Surface errors are **frequent and severe enough** to **interfere** with the reader's understanding of the work.

1 = Incompetent

The writing sample **attempts** to discuss the topic but **severely marred** because surface errors are **frequent** and **extreme**, and **severely interfere** with the reader's understanding of the work.

Scoring Guide for the SAT Writing Test

SENTENCE FORMATION AND VARIETY

6 = Clearly Competent

Sentences are **complete, grammatically correct**, and assist the reader in following the flow of the discussion. The use of a **variety** of sentence structures contributes to the effective organization of the work and the reader's understanding.

The work is **free of surface errors** (grammar, spelling, punctuation, etc.).

5 = **Reasonably Competent**

Sentences are **complete, generally correct**, and do not distract the reader from the flow of the discussion. There is evidence of a concerted effort to use a **variety** of structures.

Minor surface errors are present, but they **do not interfere** with the reader's understanding of the work.

4 = **Adequately Competent**

Sentences are **complete and generally correct**. There is evidence of a concerted effort to use a **variety** of structures.

Surface errors are present, but they **do not severely interfere** with the reader's understanding.

3 = **Nearly Competent**

Sentences are **generally complete and grammatically correct**, but there are errors that begin to distract the reader. Sentence structure might be accurate, but **dull or routine**.

Surface errors are **apparent** and **begin to interfere** with the reader's understanding of the work.

2 = **Marginally Incompetent**

Problems in **sentence structure** and **grammar** are **distracting**, and provide **little or no variety**.

Surface errors are **frequent and severe enough** to **interfere** with the reader's understanding of the work.

1 = **Incompetent**

Sentences are **riddled with errors**. There is **little or no variety** in sentence structure.

Surface errors are **frequent** and **extreme**, and **severely interfere** with the reader's understanding of the work.

Scoring Guide for the SAT Writing Test

WORD CHOICE

6 = Clearly Competent

The word choice is **specific, clear, and vivid.** Powerful nouns and verbs replace weaker adjective-noun/adverb-verb phrases. Clear, specific, and accurate words replace vague, general terms.

The work is **free of surface errors** (grammar, spelling, punctuation, etc.).

5 = Reasonably Competent

Word choice is **clear** and **accurate**. For the most part, the writer has chosen **vivid, powerful words and phrases.**

Sentences are **complete, generally correct**, and do not distract the reader from the flow of the discussion. There is evidence of a concerted effort to use a **variety** of structures.

4 = Adequately Competent

Word choice is **adequate**. For the most part, the writer has chosen **vivid, powerful words and phrases.**

Surface errors are present, but they **do not severely interfere** with the reader's understanding.

3 = Nearly Competent

Word choice is **inconsistent**.

Surface errors are **apparent** and **begin to interfere** with the reader's understanding of the work.

2 = Marginally Incompetent

Word choice is **generally vague** with a few attempts at vividness.

Surface errors are **frequent and severe enough** to **interfere** with the reader's understanding of the work.

1 = Incompetent

Word choice is **lazy, inexact**, and **vague**. The writer has either too limited a vocabulary, or has not sought the best words for the topic, audience, and purpose.

Surface errors are **frequent** and **extreme**, and **severely interfere** with the reader's understanding of the work.

Scoring Guide for the SAT Writing Test

HOLISTIC[1]

6 = Clearly Competent

The writing sample discusses the **topic effectively and insightfully**.

The paper is clearly **organized** around the central point or main idea. There is **sufficient** material (details, examples, anecdotes, supporting facts, etc.) to allow the reader to feel he/she has read a full and complete discussion without notable gaps, unanswered questions, or unexplored territory in the topic. Every word, phrase, clause, and sentence is **relevant**, contributing effectively to that idea.

The word choice is **specific, clear, and vivid.** Powerful nouns and verbs replace weaker adjective-noun/adverb-verb phrases. Clear, specific, and accurate words replace vague, general terms.

Sentences are **complete, grammatically correct**, and assist the reader in following the flow of the discussion. The use of a **variety** of sentence structures contributes to the effective organization of the work and the reader's understanding.

The work is **free of surface errors** (grammar, spelling, punctuation, etc.).

5 = Reasonably Competent

The writing sample discusses the **topic effectively**.

The **organizational plan** of the paper is **clear, but not fully implemented.** There is **nearly sufficient** material for a full and complete discussion, but the reader is left with **a few unanswered questions.** There is no superfluous or **irrelevant** material.

Word choice is **clear** and **accurate**. For the most part, the writer has chosen **vivid, powerful words and phrases.**

Minor surface errors are present, but they **do not interfere** with the reader's understanding of the work.

Sentences are **complete, generally correct**, and do not distract the reader from the flow of the discussion. There is evidence of a concerted effort to use a **variety** of structures.

[1] Adapted from materials appearing on www.collegeboard.com, the official website of the College Board.

4 = **Adequately Competent**

The writing sample **discusses the topic.**

The **organizational plan** of the paper is **apparent, but not consistently implemented.** There is **nearly sufficient** material for a full and complete discussion, but the reader is left with **a few unanswered questions.** Word choice is **adequate.** For the most part, the writer has chosen **vivid, powerful words and phrases.**

Surface errors are present, but they **do not severely interfere** with the reader's understanding.

Sentences are **complete and generally correct.** There is evidence of a concerted effort to use a **variety** of structures.

3 = **Nearly Competent**

The writing sample **discusses** the **topic** but is **marred** by the following:

There is evidence of an **organizational plan.** There are **too few** details, examples, anecdotes, supporting facts, etc.

Word choice is **inconsistent.**

Sentences are **generally complete and grammatically correct**, but there are errors that begin to distract the reader. Sentence structure might be accurate, but **dull or routine.**

Surface errors are **apparent** and **begin to interfere** with the reader's understanding of the work.

2 = **Marginally Incompetent**

The writing sample **discusses** the **topic**, but the discussion is **marred** by the following:

The **organizational plan** of the writing is obscured by **too few** details and/or **irrelevant** details.

Word choice is **generally vague** with a few attempts at vividness.

Problems in **sentence structure** and **grammar** are **distracting**, and provide **little or no variety.**

Surface errors are **frequent and severe enough** to **interfere** with the reader's understanding of the work.

1 = **Incompetent**

The writing sample **attempts** to discuss the topic but is **severely marred** by the following:

There is **no clear organizational plan** and/or **insufficient material**.

Word choice is **lazy**, **inexact**, and **vague**. The writer has either too limited a vocabulary, or has not sought the best words for the topic, audience, and purpose.

Sentences are **riddled with errors**. There is **little or no variety** in sentence structure.

Surface errors are **frequent** and **extreme**, and **severely interfere** with the reader's understanding of the work.